Save Yourself Happy

Save Yourself Happy

Easy money-saving tips for families on a budget

Gemma Bird
@moneymumofficial

hamlyn

hamlyn

First published in
Great Britain in 2022 by Hamlyn,
an imprint of
Octopus Publishing Group Ltd
Carmelite House
50 Victoria Embankment
London EC4Y 0DZ
www.octopusbooks.co.uk

An Hachette UK Company
www.hachette.co.uk

First published in paperback in
2023

ISBN 978-0-60063-735-6

A CIP catalogue record for this
book is available from the British
Library.

Printed and bound in Great
Britain.

10 9 8 7 6 5 4 3 2 1

Publishing Director: Eleanor
Maxfield
Co-author: Sarah Thompson
Senior Editor: Pauline Bache
Art Director: Yasia Williams
Designer: Jeremy Tilston
Illustrator: Abi Read
Production Manager: Caroline
Alberti

This FSC® label means that
materials used for the product have
been responsibly sourced.

The advice in this book is believed
to be correct at the time of printing,
but the authors and the publishers
accept no liability for actions
inspired by this book.

The author is not affiliated to any
financial institution. The contents
of this book do not constitute any
form of independent professional
financial advice, recommendation,
representation, endorsement or
arrangement and are not intended
to be relied upon by you in
making (or not making) a specific
investment, financial or any other
decision.

Neither the author nor
the Instagram handle,
@moneymumofficial, are related
to or associated with the charity,
MoneyMum.

Contents

Introduction. 1

Money Mum: The Story So Far. 9

Part One

Small changes, BIG savings 23

It All Adds Up. 26

Awareness Is Everything. 33

Part Two

Everybody loves a bargain – and that's OK! 47

Clothes, Fashion and Beauty 50

Homewares 61

Kids' Clothes and Toys. 64

The Food Shop. 71

Household Bills 74

Cars 80

Phones, Tech and Electronics. 83

Travelling 86

Reward Schemes 90

Other Ways to Get Discounts and Savings 93

Part Three

Money looks better in the bank than on your feet. . . . 97

Sell, Sell, Sell 100

Turning Assets into Revenue Streams 110

Put in the Hours 119

Part Four

**Stop buying things you don't need, to impress people
you don't like 129**

Identify your Money Mindset 132

When Shopping Becomes a Problem 142

Let's Talk About Debt 157

Part Five

The future's bright 171

The Art of Saving Up 174

Saving for the Big Things in Life 187

Part Six

Difficult conversations and getting the

family involved............................... 205

Building Financial Security 208

Facing Up to the Future 212

Involving the Children.......................... 222

Part Seven

Money isn't everything (and I really mean that).... 237

Financial Security 240

Mutual Support................................ 245

Gemma's Glossy Glossary 251

Index 265

Acknowledgements 271

Introduction

Money Mum here!

Welcome to my book. I can't believe I'm saying those words. When I set up my Instagram page at the start of 2019 I thought it would just be for a bit of fun, a way of sharing all my money-saving tips and a few family snaps with my friends. Now I'm writing an actual book! It's so exciting to be able to share all I've learned with you.

Because Money Mum isn't someone I've made up, just for social media. Ask anyone who knows me and they'll tell you: I really am into saving money, and I have been ever since I can remember. I guess you could say I've had to be. I wasn't academic at school and I left education when I was 16. I didn't have wealthy parents or a pot of magic money I could fall back on. I had to learn to budget and manage my wages from a very young age, and I have supported myself ever since.

I'll tell you more about my financial journey later, but first I just want to share why I am writing this book now and why I think it matters.

When I was in my thirties a close friend announced she was getting married and having her hen-do in Las Vegas. She's a good mate, one of the best, and I really, really wanted to go to Vegas and celebrate with her. But there was just no way I could afford it. I was on a low income and trying to save for a deposit on a house. I had to use a lot of my money for bills and so I'd given myself a very small budget to live on while I saved.

This was the trip of a lifetime. Vegas, baby! I wrestled with the idea of borrowing money in order to go, but I knew in my heart that I just couldn't do that. I've never borrowed and I hate the thought of being in debt, especially the kind of debt that gets bigger and bigger over time. It just seems bonkers to me, to have that hanging over you all the time. I'm a big worrier – I talk a lot about my anxiety on Instagram and later in the book – and the idea of owing large amounts of money doesn't sit well with being an anxious person. Not this one, anyway.

Truth be told, I've never really minded missing out on things if I can't afford them, and I've usually been happy to talk about my money, or lack of it. I've always been that person at the end of the night who works out the bill and only pays for what she had – sorry about that! Honestly, I've never been ashamed to be that person. For a long time I couldn't afford to be anyone else. But that hen-do was the first time I did feel kind of conflicted about addressing the issue out loud. I didn't want to let a good friend down, everyone else I knew was going, they were all finding a way and I was choosing not to. I wasn't under pressure from anyone but myself, but I still felt I was being a bad friend. More than that, I felt like I was strange for not deciding to borrow the money. I was the odd one out. The 'normal' thing to do would be to get into debt and go to the hen-do.

I want to empower women and girls to take responsibility for their own financial futures. To have those difficult conversations and do the uncomfortable maths, because, believe me, one day you will be so glad you did.

That was when it really dawned on me what a toxic culture we have around money and our finances. So many of us feel we have to pretend to be wealthier than we are and try to hide the fact we can't afford something. We borrow more and more and struggle to pay it back, and then we feel embarrassed and try to hide the truth even more. Just worrying about the hen-do made me feel bad, so I can't imagine how it must eat away at someone to be constantly struggling with debts and money worries.

I plucked up the courage, texted my friend and gave it to her straight: *I can't afford to come to Vegas and I'm not prepared to borrow money to fund it. I really hope you understand.* A few moments later the reply came in…she was absolutely fine about it! Of course she was! We went for a girls' night out in Bournemouth instead and had a brilliant night. Being upfront and honest with both myself and my friend about what I could afford paid off.

I'm in a really good place with money now. (It would be a bit strange me writing this book if I wasn't!) So much of the financial landscape has changed since then, from banking apps and bitcoin to payday loans and store cards. We are all bombarded daily with new ways to access money and new pools of credit. But when it comes down to it, there still seems to be this old-fashioned idea that money is something you don't talk about. If you've got money, you keep it a secret, and if you haven't got money, guess what? You keep it a secret!

It's a problem that affects all of us, men and women, young and old. From an early age we are being sold to – as soon as we start watching TV, adverts are telling us that we need to buy something. We grow up thinking we need to be spending money all the time. When we realise we can't, or that someone we know can buy more things than us, we start to feel inferior.

Why, though, when we are all sharing on social media what we had for our tea and how many press-ups we did that morning, can't we be more honest about our finances? Why is there still so much shame and secrecy about being a bit strapped for cash, or in debt? And why are we still ashamed to say when things are going all right? Why is saving not something we celebrate and support in our culture, instead of spending?

I feel strongly that it has to change, and I'm here to help. I am especially keen to help women take control of their finances. Even today when we see women all over the world earning more than men – absolutely smashing it in their careers, running countries and corporations – I still hear every day from girls whose partners handle the money, or who think someone else will sort it out for them. They don't

Money isn't a secret recipe that only rich people know. It's a mindset, an attitude, that anyone can have.

know who they owe for their electricity or how much they are spending a month on the mortgage, and they are in the dark about what they can and can't afford.

I want to empower women and girls to take responsibility for their own financial futures. To have those difficult conversations and do the uncomfortable maths, because, believe me, one day you will be so glad you did. What they say about death and taxes is right – we all need to know how to look after ourselves, girls! Am I right?

In this book I'll show you how to go about it – from starting small and making little changes to your everyday habits, through building a second income into your lifestyle, to going for the big goals in your life that you might think are out of your reach.

Money isn't a secret recipe that only rich people know. It's a mindset, an attitude, that anyone can have. And Money Mum is here, as always, to show you how. So put the kettle on, grab a pen and paper and let's start saving you some serious cash!

Gemma
x.
Money Mum

Money Mum:
The Story So Far

Some of my earliest memories are of saving money. Walking to junior school with my mum and little sister, Natalie, I'd scan the pavement all the way there, hanging on to Mum's hand to get as close as possible to the ground, hoping to find the odd penny or 2p that someone had dropped. If I found anything, which I did surprisingly often, I put it in an old Kenco coffee jar that I kept in the bedroom me and Natalie shared. I preferred using this to an actual piggy bank, because I could see what was inside and watch all the little brown coins multiplying over time. Occasionally I found a silver 5p, or even a 10p – they were much bigger coins in those days and really stood out from the brown pennies and 2p coins. But back then we used cash so much more, and it wasn't unusual for people to have lots of pennies in their pockets and purses; it seemed to be the pennies that got lost the most.

I kept a little piece of paper in the coffee jar and wrote on it every time I added another coin to the pot. If you've ever seen my Instagram posts, you'll know I still like to write my sums down with a pen and paper. It helps me work them out and seems to make it all clearer, and more real. Every time I found a new penny, I'd write it in the column on the left of the piece of paper and write the new total on the right. I can almost hear you laughing at this, but believe me, watching my money grow gave the young me a lot of pleasure!

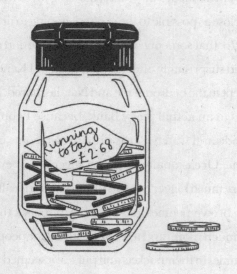

I grew up in Hertfordshire, in a two-bedroom terraced house. We weren't well off at all – Mum stayed at home and looked after us like lots of mums did in those days, and we were taught from an early age that we needed to have respect for money. When everyone at school was wearing the cool LA Gear trainers and I wanted a pair, Mum said I had to have the ones from Woolworths; when we wanted ice creams at the park, she'd make us wait until we got home and have one from the freezer. Of course, I was peeved at the time, but it taught me a valuable (pun intended) lesson: that I couldn't always have what I wanted, and that was OK. I was given an ice cream when I got home, it was just as delicious. I wore the trainers from Woolworths, my legs didn't fall off.

When I was 13, I got my first job: a paper round after school, delivering *The Evening News*, when *The Evening News* was a thing! I used to (still do) rope my best mate, Jennifer, into all my moneymaking escapades, and I made her come with me delivering the papers out of a shopping trolley I'd borrowed from an old lady down the street. This was definitely not the look Jennifer was going for at 13 years old, but I loved knowing I was earning my own cash. I had an account at the Nationwide with a little paying-in book, and I would go to pay my wages in, and watch excitedly as the book went slowly through the printer, updating the grand total.

As I got older my parents gave me an allowance: £40 a month for me to do whatever I wanted with! It was worth a lot more in those days than it is now, but it still didn't cover much. And it was meant to cover everything. It wasn't just for clothes and sweets and nice things like that, but for my bus fare, school lunches if I wanted them, make-up – everything.

In the first month I'd spent it all after about ten days. I'd been catching the bus to college every day and buying fizzy drinks and chocolate in the canteen. Then one day I really wanted to go to the cinema with Jennifer – we were keen to see *Titanic* – so I asked my dad for some cash. He asked where all my money had gone, and I explained I'd spent it all. He just looked at me and said: *Tough.*

Of course, I started complaining but I've always remembered what he said: *When you get a job, Gemma, and you've spent all your wages halfway through the month, you can't just go and ask your boss for more money because you want to go to the cinema or do whatever it is you want to do. You'll have to wait now until next month.*

And that was it. From then on, I knew I never wanted to find myself in the situation where I didn't have any money to do the things I wanted. I stopped catching the bus and started walking to school in the mornings. I didn't buy lunches and snacks from the canteen any more; I took my own in. I didn't buy loads of clothes – me and my friend Vicky used to swap things instead. I realised I could make things last a lot longer than most people did, and not only that – I was really good at saving.

I'd never been academic at school – I loved singing and dancing and wanted to be a performer. Academic subjects never came easy to me, especially maths, believe it or not. So, at 16, I left school and got a job at my local medical centre, hoping to go to auditions in my evenings and weekends. (This was before *The X Factor* and *The Voice*, when you got a copy of *The Stage* and you queued up outside the theatres for an audition.) My wages were £1,000 a month. Although my parents couldn't give me money for a deposit on a house, they said that if I could save for it, they wouldn't charge me housekeeping. That was how they helped me and I have always been grateful.

There's this money-saving motto you might have heard: spend half, save half. People reckon if you want to pay off your big debts or save for something important like a deposit on a house, you've got to be putting at least half of your income away every month. Saving 50 per cent wasn't enough for me, I saved 80 per cent and lived on 20 per cent. Every month I put £800 in the bank and lived on £200, giving myself £50 a week. It was amazing how quickly it added up. I even remember the lady in the Nationwide saying how well I was doing!

Around that time all my friends started going out to nightclubs, and as soon as I'd passed my driving test I always offered to drive. I've never been into drinking, so it wasn't a big sacrifice for me to say I'd have a lime and soda. And most of the time someone would buy me that because I was the one driving! People thought I'd be bored but I wasn't – I always danced and had a great time *and* I didn't waste loads of cash on a night out that I couldn't remember in the morning.

I suppose you could say it became a kind of addiction, a challenge every month, to get through to the end with my savings in the bank and cash in my hand. I enjoyed it. I still do – I wouldn't be writing this book if I didn't! Looking back, I realise I was quite unusual for a teenager. Everyone I knew was getting money from their parents and spending all their cash as fast as they could get hold of it. But I think the fact I never minded saying upfront that I wasn't going to be spending money that day, or didn't want to buy this or that – I was willing to miss out on things I couldn't pay for – made a big difference. When someone tries to hide the fact that they don't have the cash, or they feel ashamed to say they're on a budget, that's when people start calling them tight or mean. But where I was just straight-up, bold – *I'm saving for a deposit,*

I'm not paying for that or *I can't afford to go* – I think my friends and the people around me very quickly got on board with it. They were like, *Oh, that's just Gemma.* (I talk about people's attitudes to money and why there's no shame in saving on page 132.)

It paid off. By the time I was 17 I'd bought my first car and by the time I was 23 I had saved enough money, along with my then-partner, for a deposit on my first house. I kept on saving, and three years later I had enough money to go in with my dad on a couple of buy-to-let properties (back when you could get a buy-to-let mortgage with a low deposit). I always overpaid my mortgage repayments, we let the spare room at our house and we just did everything we could to get the mortgage down. Things didn't work out with my first husband in the end, and when we sold the house I moved back in with my mum and dad. As I've never really drunk alcohol, instead of going to the pub in the evenings I worked there, and I took on extra work as a driving instructor (I love driving!) on top of my day job, which at the time was an estate agent. My dad and I sold the two properties we'd bought together, and by the time I met Adam in 2010, I'd got enough money behind me to go in with him on the house he lived in: I basically paid off the outstanding amount on his mortgage. And that's the home where we live now, with our children Brody and Bronte.

I'm a columnist for a national newspaper, and in articles in that paper and in other press I've talked a bit about how I came to be mortgage-free. A lot of the feedback was positive and people – especially young people and women – were keen to hear about how I'd done it. They were really supportive of everything I'd achieved. But I was also pretty shocked by how much negative feedback I got, people who said I'd obviously been bought a house by my dad or had moved into Adam's without paying my share. No! I worked hard to get to this point and I have never expected a man to buy me anything! I'll talk more about the perils of social media and the anxiety of criticism later (see page 151), but this was the first time I realised how we don't talk positively enough about people who are doing well for themselves, especially if they happen to be women.

That said, I wouldn't be Money Mum without Adam, aka Money Dad. He supports me in everything, looks after the kids when I'm working, takes care of all the paperwork – he's there for all of us all the time. And as you would expect, he loves to save as well! I think it's so important, when you are looking for a partner, to find someone with the same values at their core, and Adam is just like me. He was raised to respect money; we both hate wasting it and we both love a bargain! More importantly, we communicate and talk about our finances – it's something we do together.

I won't pretend it has always been easy. Having been a massive worrier all my life, I know that a big part of my compulsion to save stems from my problems with overthinking and feeling anxious. When everything around you feels like it is out of your control, saving money is something you *can* control. For some people, dealing with anxiety is about cleaning rituals or addictive substances, but for me it's saving! It's something I've lived with for most of my adult life, and if you follow me on Instagram you'll know I have good days and bad days. I overthink things, I worry about who likes me and who doesn't, I imagine situations that may or may not happen. My mind goes into overdrive and I can feel either really fraught and strung out, or else like I just can't cope. I don't mind telling people this, especially when I'm feeling a bit low. I don't want my social media image to be a one-dimensional, everything-is-perfect person. I always think anxiety is a bit like money – we should all be talking a lot more about it and not feel ashamed to say when times are hard. As the old saying goes, a problem shared is a problem halved. It's so true. Almost as soon as you tell someone about what's bothering you, it lifts, doesn't it?

You might think that because I'm in a good place now, with my family and Instagram page and Adam, the anxiety might have gone, or at least receded. But anyone with anxiety will tell you that it doesn't go away when the things you are worrying about go away! It just finds new things for you to worry about. Sometimes I even get worried if I'm not worried! That's how sneaky anxiety can be.

In fact, one of my biggest personal challenges at this point is learning to relax about it and take my foot off the savings pedal. I still want to save it all! Adam always says behaviour is the hardest thing to change, and he's right – I don't think I've really changed the way I am around money ever since I started saving all those years ago.

I do have a lot more peace of mind these days. I can treat my kids to more stuff when we are out and about than my parents ever could, and we've been on some lovely family holidays. But I still don't buy them ice creams every time they ask for one or give them loads of expensive gifts at Christmas. My happiest memories are of time spent with my mum in the park or the library – simple, free fun, because childhood shouldn't come with a price tag – and that's what I want for my kids.

I started posting on Instagram in 2019. A friend showed me what she'd been doing on it and I thought it sounded fun. I guess it appealed to the performer in me! I love a good chinwag and I was up for doing little videos and chatting to people. I thought about what I could say on there, what my 'schtick' was going to be. I'd got a reputation with my friends as the one who always had the voucher codes and the discounts – everyone knew I was well up for a bargain or a deal. And by that stage I was already mortgage-free; not many people I knew had done that by my age. Instagram sounded like a way for me to talk about all that I'd learned, giving advice and tips in a more organised way. And because I always liked to get the family involved – Bronte had just been born at that point – I could post a few pics of them on there as well. More importantly, it was a low-risk venture

– Instagram is free. I had nothing to lose and everything to gain. So I picked up my phone and got to work.

Hundreds of thousands of followers, one national newspaper column and a whole load of fun later, here I am, writing this book, sharing it all with you, so you can start saving yourself happy too! Let's get cracking!

I always think anxiety is a bit like money – we should all be talking a lot more about it and not feel ashamed to say when times are hard.

Part One

Small changes,
BIG savings

We've all heard it a hundred times or more: look after the pennies and the pounds will look after themselves. And you know what? It is so true!

Often we talk about penny-pinching and people being tight, or we say people know their way around a pound note (or we used to say that, back when there *were* pound notes!) to imply that someone is mean with their money. But looking after the pennies doesn't have to involve being stingy or unkind. That's why it's called 'looking after' – it's about taking care of your money, showing it a bit of love and attention, rather than being tight.

Believe me, I'm not about depriving yourself or going without. I love the nice things in life – I live in Essex, after all! But I firmly believe that real wealth is when you can *afford* all the things, not buy them on credit or get yourself into debt to have a lifestyle you can't pay for. And like anything worth waiting for, that kind of 'rich' only comes when you start to value the small things, taking notice of all the little costs here and there.

When you start looking after the pennies, the innocent everyday costs that you think don't matter, the tenner here or the quid there – and we'll come to what those costs are made up of shortly – that's when you start to be in charge of your money. And being in control, knowing what you can and can't afford, making decisions that are good for you, your family and your future, that is the saver's mindset we are after. It might not be an instant fix, but when it comes to making big bucks, you've got to start thinking like the tortoise, not the hare.

The great thing about making small changes is this: it doesn't matter what you earn, and you don't need to be rich or have a high salary to start making real savings and seeing results. How come? Because here's the thing: saving isn't just about what's coming in, it's also about what's going out! Once you realise this, it's like a lightbulb coming on. Make that mental switch in your mind now, and you'll start noticing how you can save money pretty much every day, and everywhere you go. How does it work? I'm going to show you how.

When it comes to making big bucks, you've got to start thinking like the tortoise, not the hare.

It All Adds Up

What do I mean by the everyday things and small changes?
Well, putting the big household bills like energy and council
tax aside for a moment, just think about all the things we
spend our money on, every single day.

From the minute we wake up, we might listen to music

that we're paying a subscription for, have a shower with products we like to use, do our make-up, put on our favourite perfume, head off to work and buy a coffee and magazine for the journey. Even before we've arrived at work, we've probably spent half a day's wages. How scary is that?

Simply by looking a little bit closer at these everyday costs, the ones we sometimes don't even notice, we can start to make savings. Here are a few examples to get you started:

Coffees on the go

This is a great way to start noticing more cash in your pocket or bank account straightaway. Everyone loves a cuppa first thing, especially on the way to work – the waft of fresh coffee is hard to beat. But the average medium latte costs around £3, which means that if you have one every morning, you are spending £15 a week on coffee! That's before you've thrown in a snack or picked up another one at lunchtime or on the way home. Look at what you could save in a year simply by ditching the morning coffees:

£3 x 5 = £15

£15 a week = £60 a month over 12 months = £720

> **DO THIS:** Use a flask or travel mug to start taking your own coffee to work. You'll buy yourself more time in the morning (no more queuing in Costa) and see extra cash in your account without even trying.

Subscriptions

Do you know how many subscriptions you have? Not just your ordinary subscriptions like gym membership or your TV package, but all the apps you pay monthly for. Maybe it's news, a music streaming service, beauty buying club, meditation app, fitness app, supermarket discount pass, pet food. Now ask yourself honestly, do you use them all? Can you even remember what they all are?

So many subscription-based services lure you in by offering you a free trial or a low introductory rate, and the promise of convenience, like never having to think about the cat's flea treatment again. But all too often you forget that the free trial has to be cancelled, or that your introductory rate of £3 a month is going up to £25, and by the time you do remember it's too late. You've already spent £100 and got nothing to show for it, apart from four months of flea treatments you haven't even used on the cat yet.

Whatever it is you've signed up for, unless it is 100 per cent essential (and I have to say, I'm struggling to think of what it could be that you can't go out and buy if you really need it), a subscription is the definition of money for old rope. Your cash is automatically going out of your account every month and it may be for a service you're not even using. Excuse me? Companies are making money from people who don't use their services and often don't even notice they are spending money on them!

Do it now, while you remember: go and look at all your subscriptions and add up how much you are spending every month on them. I'll bet you find a few you'd forgotten about, and I guarantee you'll be surprised by how much it is costing you every month. Now cancel them all! You can always sign up again if you find you're missing them. But I have a hunch you won't be.

Kids' treats and toys

How many of us buy little treats for our kids when we are out and about, just to keep them busy or calm down a tantrum? And how many of us have duplicates of the same toys, because we know our kids like them? So often I see children's toy boxes full of the same toys, whether it's ten Barbie dolls or twenty Hot Wheels cars. It's madness!

Have you heard of toy rotation? Basically, you keep a few of your children's toys hidden away and every few days you get them out and hide some of the ones that have been out for a while. Children don't care about the packaging or if something is from a shop – they just like the novelty of having a 'new' toy to play with for a bit. It also means less tat around the place for you to clean up at the end of the day!

It's easy to rotate their toys at home, and with a bit of forward thinking you can make it work for you when you are out and about. Just pop a car, a puzzle or a play figure they haven't seen for a while in your handbag, and then when a new distraction is needed – ta-dah! It will buy you the time and the peace you need, without costing you a thing.

Another thing to remember when you're out and about is that supermarkets put sweets and chocolate on display by the tills because they know your kids will be getting restless by the time you get to the checkout and you'll do anything to keep them quiet. And they are always so expensive!

As a mum I know how hard it can be to say no to children, especially if they are whingeing in public and everyone is watching! But once they realise that you're not going to budge on this, they will accept that these sweets are not going to happen and will stop asking. In child psychology this is called 'planned ignoring'. The idea is that you ignore the 'bad' behaviour and eventually it goes away. (This isn't the same as just ignoring your child, which I'm not saying is a good idea!) Ignoring kids' tantrums, as well as quietly explaining that this is what is happening and why, can help you get past those moments in the supermarket when it feels like you've got to buy them this or that just to keep them quiet. The same goes for children's magazines with plastic toys on the cover, and the rides by the toilets. They all cost so much and children have forgotten them in two minutes. Definitely not worth the money. Remember, saving is not only about what's coming in, it's also about what's going out.

So, we've looked at some of the main areas where our everyday spending can be cut back. I guarantee you can find plenty more ways to save on the small things – it all depends on your lifestyle and what you spend your money on.

DO THIS: Have a think about what other areas of your day-to-day routine you can save on. Write it all down and keep it handy, because in a minute you can add it to your new spending tracker.

Saving is not only about what's coming in, it's also about what's going out.

Awareness Is Everything

Now that you've started really thinking about how to make small savings, the chances are you have already become more aware of where your money is going and how much is going out. So give yourself a pat on the back, because it's not always easy to face the truth, especially if it means admitting you've been overspending or wasting money. As Adam says, even those little changes can be difficult not only to make, but also to maintain.

That's where I come in!

Once you've started to realise where all your hard-earned cash is going, you'll need encouragement and support to stay on the right track. I've got three simple tricks to keep you going and help make those small changes stick. In no time, we'll have you moving from being someone who spends to being someone who saves.

Use my Hourly Rate Principle

If you get paid by the hour, this shouldn't be too hard for you to work out! But even if you don't – maybe you're self-employed or you have an annual salary – it's easy enough to work out your hourly rate: what you get paid for an hour of your time.

To do this, divide your annual earnings by 52 to get your weekly income. (Make sure it's your earnings after you've paid your tax and National Insurance.) Now divide your weekly income by the number of hours you work. (If your hours are variable, use an average figure – the average national working week is 40 hours.) That gives you your hourly rate of pay. Here's a simple example:

Annual salary £20k divided by 52 = £385 a week

£385 divided by 35 = £11 an hour

This doesn't need to be precise or accurate, as it's only an estimate. The point is you are trying to get a rough idea of how much money you earn every hour.

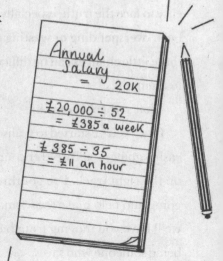

Annual
Salary
= 20k

£20,000 ÷ 52
= £385 a week

£385 ÷ 35
= £11 an hour

Because once you have that figure in your mind, you can begin to ask yourself not only if you can afford it, but if what you are about to buy or order is worth an hour of your life.

Here's an example: let's say you work out that you earn £11 an hour, and you agree to meet a friend for tea in the park on your day off. By the time you buy a tea and a bit of cake in the café, you will have spent around £5. If you offer to pay for your friend, it might be more like £10. If you've got the kids with you and they want a drink and a bit of cake as well, you might end up spending £15 minimum.

That's over an hour of your working day, just to buy some hot water with a teabag in it and get a taste of something sweet!

Now ask yourself why you are going to meet your friend. Is it because you really like the tea at that café in the park, or is it to see them and have a good natter? If it's to see them, why not take your own tea in a flask and pack some biscuits in a Tupperware box from the tin at home? You'll save money and you'll still enjoy all the nice things about going to the park.

What's it worth?

This little exercise is for you to do with your friends or children or just by yourself. It will help you get a real sense of what your hourly rate is, and how you can apply it to your everyday life.

Draw a table with three columns, and in the left-hand column write a list of the top ten 'little things' you spend money on. Not your bills or mortgage or car, but all those incidental, non-essential spends like buying coffees or having your nails done. What it is will depend on you and your lifestyle. Here's an example:

Gel nails		
Coffee at the station		
Cleansing wipes		
Renting movie on Amazon		
Takeaway on Friday		
Ice creams for kids		
Cab fare		
Blow-dry		
Drink after work		
Wax melts		

In the second column write down how much work time, according to your hourly rate, each little thing costs you. It could be that your hourly rate is £10 and buying two coffees is £5, so it is costing you half an hour at the office simply to buy them.

In the third column put a tick or a cross to show how you feel about whether it is worth it. Would you rather be in the office doing overtime to buy the coffees, or in the park with your children and your own coffee that you brought from home? Don't think too hard about it – just go with your gut feeling. Those ticks (for good) and crosses (for bad) will help you to see whether what you are spending your money on is the best use of your time, or whether you're just doing it without thinking.

Keep the HRP (Hourly Rate Principle) in mind every time you go online or are out shopping. Get into the habit of asking yourself if what you are about to spend is worth another hour of work. Often, you'll find it's not worth it, and what's more, you'll feel proud of yourself for walking away from it. Notice the change: instead of feeling that you are missing out, you'll begin to feel strong and start believing in your ability to save money.

Track your spending

So many people roll their eyes at this because they think it sounds boring. But there is nothing boring about going on an amazing holiday or buying yourself a new car. Am I right?

A spending tracker is easy to set up and you'll only have to do it once. When it's up and running, you'll find you want to use it more and more. It's kind of like being in a saving competition with yourself, and this is the scoreboard.

How does it work?

If you've got a computer you can use a programme like Excel or Google Sheets, which is great because it does all the calculations for you. But if you don't have access to a computer or you prefer using pen and paper, you can write it down instead. I know some people who use a whiteboard in the kitchen for this. It's up to you how you do it – the important thing is that you are keeping a record of your spending and your income every month.

1 Write down all your expected monthly outgoings in one column: mortgage, bills, food shop, pension, everything. Don't worry about being totally accurate, just get it down.

Top Tip: If you're not sure, make an educated guess and write a projection. You can come back to it when you have an actual figure. For example, I always put in a rough figure for clothes because I know someone is going to need some shoes or a new bra or whatever it is that month, even though I may not know yet exactly what the costs will be. You can amend these figures later – it's not homework and no one is going to be marking it!

---

2 In another column, write down what you have got coming in that month: wages, any tax credits, refunds you might be expecting, birthday money, a bonus. Put down literally everything you are expecting to land in your bank account.

3 Add up your outgoings column and also add up your income column. Now subtract your outgoings from your income and see what you have left.

This figure is what you need to keep at the front of your mind when you are about to buy yourself a new top or an overpriced hot dog at the cinema. It's not about how much the item costs, it's about whether you can afford it. A simple spending tracker like this will help you decide if you can.

Remember, it's not about what something costs, it's about whether you can afford it.

Spending tracker

Money In	
Monthly Salary	
Tax Credits	
Bonus	
Total In	£££

Money Out	
Mortgage	
Council Tax	
TV	
Water	
Broadband	
Electric & Gas	
ISA	
Kids' ISA	
Pension	
Mobile	
Credit Card	
Car Insurance	
Petrol	
Groceries	
Clothes	
Family Days Out	
School Dinner Money	
Life Insurance	
Total Out	£££

Net Total (of Ins minus Outs)	£££
Overall Monthly Surplus	£££

Try my No Spend Day

I set up this challenge during the first lockdown of the Covid-19 pandemic, in summer 2020. It was a time of real uncertainty and it seemed to me like everyone I knew was worried about money and job security – no one knew what was going to happen or how life would look when the pandemic was over. We were seeing images of empty supermarket shelves and people queuing up for food, and it felt quite scary and surreal.

My Instagram numbers had been steadily growing. I think I had something like 10,000 followers by then, which seemed unimaginable to me. I noticed I had followers coming from all walks of life – it wasn't only mums or young people who were interested in saving money. It felt like I had really struck a chord with all sorts of people, from dads and grandparents to teenagers and mums.

I wanted to find a way to help my followers save a bit of money: a kind of community thing that everyone on my Instagram could get involved with and feel like they were doing something positive during the pandemic. One morning I was doing my make-up and it just came to me: get everyone doing a No Spend Day!

I had been doing No Spend Days for myself ever since I could remember. In the early days when I was really saving hard for a deposit, I would sometimes do three or four No Spend Days a week! But I realised that even if everyone just did one day a week it would make such a difference to their bank balance. More importantly, it would get them into the habit of saving and being a bit more aware of where their money was going.

I launched #gemmasnospendday and was immediately blown away by how many people got involved and shared all the savings they had made, simply by committing not to spend for one single day in the week. Loads of followers posted videos talking about some of the things they *hadn't* spent money on that day. It was so refreshing and exciting to see!

The technique for No Spend Day is pretty simple – you just don't spend any money for a day! If you're hanging out with friends, you go round each other's house rather than meeting in town where you'll spend money. If you're doing something with the kids, it has to be free, like going to the park or doing drawing at home. You take your own coffees instead of going to the café. You definitely don't buy any new clothes or get your nails done or do anything that costs money! Even food shopping is out: instead, be creative with what you already have in the cupboard.

Quite a few of my friends do it now as a regular thing, and I love to see that. My business partner in **BB Lingerie**, Louise (@mrsmissinstyle), posted that she had avoided going to **BM Stores** and Home Bargains and had done her own nails. Another friend, @chantellechamps, who posts about her life with three daughters (including twins), met up with me for the day at the beach, and the kids just had the best day, with not a penny spent. One mum (@thehighfieldboys) who has three boys (also including twins) posted that they'd made a bonfire and toasted marshmallows in the garden. How cute is that?

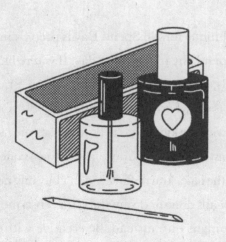

It's amazing to see how creative and resourceful you can be when you know you can't spend any money. And if you want to take my No Spend Day to the next level, you can add up all the money you have saved by not spending and then put it into your savings account.

Top Tip: **You could involve your friends and family by setting up a No Spend Day group on WhatsApp, or get the kids on board and ask them to add up all your savings on No Spend Day. They'll discover that things don't always just fall in your lap, and it will help them learn to save.**

Part Two

Everybody loves a bargain
– and that's OK!

Now that you have started to think about the small changes you can make to see big savings in your everyday life, you can begin to look at how to spend your hard-won money that little bit smarter, and make even more savings. Why? Because more savings equals more of the things you want in life!

Believe it or not, I do like having nice things. I'm not here to be a bore and tell you that you don't need a big house or a new car or that you don't have to go on amazing holidays. Quite the opposite. In fact, I'd say those three things are the most important symbols of achievement to me. (People are always surprised by how much I like a nice car!) I really value owning my home because it's where I feel safe and at peace with my family, and my car because I spend a lot of time in it and I enjoy getting out and about – it makes me feel free! I love my holidays because that's where I can get the things money can't buy: love and time with my family.

Whatever is important to you, you can pretty much guarantee that having enough money to do it makes it all the more sweet. So this chapter is all about making space for those extra funds, spending less on the things you really *don't* want to be spending it on, like household bills, the supermarket shop, car insurance and even your clothes, so there's more for all the things you *do* want in life.

Whatever is important to you, you can pretty much guarantee that having enough money to do it makes it all the more sweet.

Clothes, Fashion and Beauty

You might expect me to tell you not to buy yourself too many clothes and to make do and mend if you want to save money. You can definitely make some savings in the clothing department by looking after your threads a bit more: hang them up, steam them instead of washing them all the time and alter things if they don't fit you. Clothes are so disposable these days, it's crazy what we throw out. But you don't need me to tell you any of that – I might be Money Mum, but I'm not your actual mum!

Me and clothes shopping: a love story

What I *can* help with is teaching you a few tricks to help bring the cost of your clothes shopping down. Because I love clothes and I love shopping! I have always enjoyed going round the shops, even if it's just window-shopping. Which, let's be honest, it was for me for a very long time. As a kid, hanging out with my friends at the shops after school was what we did. I was always in and out of them, and always coveting something.

I remember the first item of clothing I really wanted was a pair of black leggings with the low rise at the front and flared bottoms that went over your trainers. OMG I loved that look! I worked two jobs at the weekends, one in a greengrocer's and the other in a CD shop, and saved up to buy myself a pair. (I got a belly-bar piercing as well, blimey that hurt. I've still got the hole!) But even then, I did my research and went into all the shops every day after school to check out which leggings were best, which had the best price and whether any had been put on sale. I can safely say that I have never been an impulse purchaser.

These days I still love shopping for clothes and buying nice things for my home. And in many ways I haven't really changed my approach from when I was a teenager. I still do lots of research and I still make sure I've got the best deal I possibly can before I buy anything.

But as I get older, I find I'm less interested in high fashion and instead try to buy just a couple of 'fashion' pieces (which tend to be the most fleeting and the most expensive items) each season, and keep the rest of my clothes fairly simple and versatile. I still enjoy a good haul at H&M or Primarni! And even with the expensive pieces I'll always try to get a bargain. I save searches for all my favourite brands on eBay, so I can buy pieces second-hand (there is more about eBay on page 104). My cherished Gucci handbag I got from a designer outlet shopping village for a third of the retail price, but it was still quite a lot to spend on a bag. I felt a bit sick handing over my card that day, let me tell you, but I consoled myself with knowing I was getting such a whopping discount.

What are designer shopping villages and are they worth it?

There are around 80 designer outlet shopping villages around the UK, and they are a great way to pick up big discounts on otherwise expensive high fashion and homewares. Top designers like Armani, Dunhill and Michael Kors sell off surplus stock from their recent seasons, with discounts of up to 60 per cent on the recommended retail price, making them handy for big purchases like handbags, watches and winter coats. Not all villages are the same, though – some are more focussed on high-street brands while others are big on designer labels. Check the store list before you go, to see if the brands you want are there. And make sure what you are buying is an authentic discounted last-season piece, not something that has been made exclusively for the outlet, which can sometimes be the case. Know the product you are looking for and talk to the staff there if you have any concerns. They might even offer you a longer return period or a bigger discount!

I'm also a big fan of all the new fashion rental schemes that are available now, especially if there's a wedding or a special occasion coming up. Carrie Johnson got married in a rented wedding dress, and if it's good enough for the Prime Minister's wife, it's good enough for me. There are loads of different brands and apps offering various approaches to fashion rental: with some, you just hire one-off pieces as you want them, while others offer a subscription and give you a selection of clothes every month. Just make sure you factor in all the postage and any cleaning charges, as sometimes it might be more effective to buy the piece and resell it or rent it out yourself (see pages 104 and 113 for more on selling and renting out your unwanted clothing).

Top Tip: **Research carried out on behalf of the Royal Society of Arts (RSA) in 2020 found that during the pandemic, 28 per cent of people were recycling or reusing more clothes than previously and 35 per cent of women said they intended to buy fewer clothes in the future. Renting one-off pieces is hands-down better for the planet as it involves less energy to produce one amazing dress than it does a whole truckload. If you want to make sure your rentals are as ethical as possible, check what your rental service has to say about delivery and packaging, as these can also make a big impact on your fashion carbon footprint. It might seem unimportant but, as with saving money, saving the planet starts with the small things.**

If you like window-shopping, you might think that you'll have to miss out on this favourite pastime to maximise your money saving. While it might seem like window-shopping is about looking longingly at something you really want and can't afford, it can also be something to enjoy in its own right, regardless of whether you've got money to spend at that time or not. Many high-street shops are such incredible spaces these days – created by top interior designers, often with highly curated brand soundtracks, they have loads of interesting things to look at (especially the people). If you can let go of the idea that you have to purchase something, just being in that space can be fun, like going to an art gallery or a museum. The bigger and grander the shop, the more interesting the things to see. It's no coincidence that the Christmas windows at top London department stores like Harvey Nichols and Selfridges are always so amazing. They know that by creating visually stunning windows, they'll draw people in.

Window-shopping is also a great way to work out if you really want something or not. Things on display in the shops can be very alluring, but once you get home you may find you don't really want it as much as you did when you were in the shop. Treat your window-shopping as a kind of testing process. If you love something while you are window-shopping but you get home and find that you have forgotten about it after a while, the chances are it wasn't for you in the first place.

Window-shopping is a good opportunity to research. Whether you are thinking about a new summer look or working on a mood board for your wedding, shops are spilling over with ideas that you can steal and put your own twist on. Take plenty of pictures of the things you like while you are out and about and you'll have an instant file for inspiration. By approaching your purchases this way, you start to feel more in control, and you buy things when you are ready, not because you have your head turned in a moment of weakness!

Top Tip: **Instagram and other social media are really an extension of window-shopping in that you can scroll through and see how other people do up their houses or what clothes they wear, without having to buy anything. I used to love following Lisa Vanderpump and getting all her home interior ideas, then I'd go to The Range or Homebase and pick up cheaper versions. My picture frames weren't silver but they were silver-coloured!**

Shopping for clothes dos and don'ts:

- Don't buy on impulse.
- Enjoy window-shopping as an activity in itself.
- Research, research, research.
- Check out rental options.
- Follow your favourite stars for style inspiration, then buy cheaper.
- Buy the big, expensive pieces second-hand or at shopping outlets.
- Save searches on eBay for all your favourite brands and items.

Hair and beauty products

How many half-finished tubs of body lotion, cans of hairspray and other unused products do you reckon are sitting in your bathroom and bedroom cupboards right now?

We all spend so much on beauty products. Time was, all you needed was a bottle of baby lotion and some cotton wool pads and you were good to go! Now we use serums and night creams and eye creams and cleansing waters…I've lost track of what they all do!

I'm not here to tell you what you need and don't need for

your beauty regime – we all know what works for us and what doesn't. But just a few simple changes can help you spend less on these things over time, which means putting more of your money into the bank. That will make you sleep better, and we all know beauty sleep is the best thing for a great complexion, right?

- Make them last longer. Put the lids back on and squeeze out every last drop of your products, whether they are toothpaste or hair remover. Those last drops might mean extra money in the bank, and it's better there than in the bathroom bin. A freezer-bag clip at the bottom of a tube is a great way to make sure you are getting everything out.·

Top Tip: **Put them in the fridge! Did you know that storing nail varnish, lipsticks and other make-up in the fridge keeps them fresher for longer? This might not work for the products you use all the time, but if you've got an eye-shadow set you only use for nights out or a lipstick that you use more in the winter than the summer, pop them in the fridge and they'll be good to go next time you want to wear them!**

- Use up what you've got first. This is so obvious. What's the point of buying more shampoo when you have a load sitting in the cupboard? Why give your money to the shops instead of keeping it in your bank? Go and get everything out of the cupboards and see what you've got that you can use up before you spend any more. If you've got half-used bottles of shampoo that you no longer want to use every day but haven't thrown away, decant them into travel bottles and you've got instant toiletries for your holidays and work trips.

- Educate yourself. So much of the beauty industry is about branding and packaging, so take some time to understand what's in your favourite products, and see if you can find the same thing cheaper, under a different brand name. You will be shocked! Especially with some things like micellar water, which you really don't need to be buying expensive versions of. If you can't bear to have the wrong packaging out on the side, pour your budget version into an old container of your favourite brand, and enjoy knowing you've still got all the good bits for half the price.

Homewares

Home is my happy place, it's where my family comes together, where we celebrate, relax, spend downtime and generally feel safe. It won't come as a surprise that I like doing my house up and making it look nice! You'll see from my Instagram pictures that I like all the neutral shades and tones like whites and greys and beiges – I think they look elegant and timeless – and I like to mix them up with lots of different textures such as fluffy cushions and silver mirrors to make it interesting.

But as you'd expect, I've never shopped at the expensive homeware stores. I've always found cheaper pieces that don't cost as much from discount shops like B&M and Homesense. I then mix them up with second-hand finds and do them up myself with a lick of paint or new fabrics.

I've also learned the art of tweaking a few key features here and there to create a fresh look, instead of giving the room a whole makeover. It's amazing how just switching the print in a frame or changing the handles on a chest of drawers can make a room feel different instantly, without spending loads of money on a decorator.

Makeover ideas

Whatever your style, there is simply no need to fork out a fortune on new stuff for your house. Here are some of my favourite money-saving makeover ideas:

- Find furniture at car boot sales or charity shops, and upcycle it with your favourite colours and new accessories like handles and knobs.

- Paint old leather chairs and sofas with chalk paint instead of buying new ones (yes, you can paint leather!). Chalk paint is amazing as it goes on easily and you don't have to prepare surfaces like you would with regular paint.

- Decide on a colour scheme and stick to it – it makes shopping for pieces easier. You are less likely to make expensive mistakes if everything is in the same tonal range.

- Buy picture frames and furniture in neutral colours, then you can just change the fabrics or the pictures if you want to do something different. The same goes for lamps – you can simply change the shade or spray it a new colour instead of buying a whole new lamp.

- Skill-up! There are tutorials online for just about everything these days. Learn the tricks of the trade and save yourself a fortune by doing your own decorating and simple DIY jobs.

- Personalisation is a brilliant way to make furniture look unique and interesting. Stencil your children's names on their toy boxes and wardrobes and you get an instant upgrade.

- Instead of redecorating a whole room, freshening up accessories like cushions and blankets can sometimes be all you need to do.

- The same applies to simply moving the furniture around.

- Painting doors or replacing them is also a great way to create a whole new feel for less cost than doing a complete room.

- If your carpet is worn out and you know you've got wooden floorboards under it, you could try painting or varnishing them instead of getting new carpet.

- Fancy wallpaper is expensive, so a feature wall is a good way to get a little bit of interest going without spending thousands at Farrow & Ball.

Kids' Clothes and Toys

If you follow me on Instagram, you'll know how much I love dressing my children. It has been one of the most entertaining aspects of being a mum, seeing Bronte in a pink tutu and a big bow in her hair or Brody looking cool in his jeans and high-tops. But even though my kids always look smart, you'll never find me spending a fortune on their clothes. It's just not worth it when they grow out of them so fast. They do have the odd designer outfit, but that's usually for my benefit, not theirs! Kids don't care what they are wearing, do they? And if they're in Primarni instead of Armani, you spend a lot less time worrying about whether they are getting dirty and spoiling their fun.

As you'd expect, I get a lot of their things on eBay and other second-hand marketplaces, especially the big stuff like winter coats. I love Moncler jackets and I have bought Brody one every winter for the last few years and then resold it when he's grown out of it. It's an expensive brand but that's because

Kids don't care what they are wearing, do they? And if they're in Primarni instead of Armani, you spend a lot less time worrying about whether they are getting dirty and spoiling their fun.

it's such good quality, so the pieces hold their value. I have even sold one of his jackets for more than I paid for it!

And, of course, I try to get as much as possible of their school uniforms second-hand. My kids' school has a Facebook group for second-hand where you can see what's available and post your own stuff. Some schools have a rail in reception and others do proper uniform sales. I know it's not possible to always get their whole uniform second-hand, but if you can aim for at least 50 per cent of it, you will be saving yourself a lot of money. Especially on things they don't wear all the time, like sports gear, or if, like mine, your children have a habit of losing things.

The same goes for me with kids' toys, especially at Christmas and birthdays. I have a rule about Christmas stockings – I only buy them one 'real' present and the rest are little things from Poundland or charity shops. I know they will start to notice when they get older, but while they are small there really is no need to be spending a fortune on stocking fillers that they play with for five minutes and then forget about. I put some money in their bank accounts instead. I know they'll be grateful for that when the time comes.

Here are some other ideas for saving on your kids' bits and bobs:

- Organise informal clothing swaps between a few of your

friends. If you can find a friend with children who are the right age and whose clothes you like, you can share and swap their outfits for years!

- Check your local charity shops. I always pop into the ones nearest the poshest parts of town, as you get better-quality things in there.

- Set a rule for what you will spend at Christmas and birthdays, and stick to it. Otherwise it can get out of hand and your children come to expect too much.

- Borrow toys from toy libraries rather than buying new.

- Buy school blazers and coats a size up so they last for two years rather than one.

We need to talk about parties

Children do not need expensive birthday parties! I am continually gobsmacked by how much people spend on massive, showy parties for small children who don't even remember them when they are older! I see it all the time: expensive venues and food no one eats, wine and drinks for the grown-ups (er, it's a kids' party) and party bags that cost more than the present you gave the birthday girl or boy!

I've been to enough children's parties to know that children only need a few basics from a birthday party in order to feel that they have had the time of their lives. Provide these things and you are giving them the best belter of a birthday party *ever*, I promise:

- Party games. You don't need to hire an entertainer or put on a rave! Good old-fashioned pass-the-parcel and musical statues are still the best fun for young children and cost very little to do. (And no, you don't need to put a sweet in every layer of the parcel they pass!) If you don't feel comfortable being the games master, ask your bubbliest friend if they'll do you a favour. You can always help them out with their party next time.

- Party food, by which I mean a few sandwiches or some pizza, sweets and biscuits and jelly and ice cream. Yes, we all know you are a good mum and want to give them healthy tomatoes and carrot sticks, but I can confirm that no one eats the tomatoes at a birthday party! Save your money and let them eat cake all day.

- Space to run around in. If it's the summer, then your garden or the park is a great place to have a party. Make some paper bunting with the kids, hang it in the trees or around the patio and, ta-dah, you have a party zone. If it's winter and you don't want to be in your home, try your local village hall or community centre. They are usually cheap to rent out by the hour and have kitchens/facilities for making food and washing up. The important thing is that there is space to play games and burn off all that cake!

- A birthday cake with candles. Again, you don't need to reconstruct Wembley Stadium in cake form for your five-year-old's birthday party. You especially don't need to spend a fortune on getting someone else to do it for you. It's blowing out the candles and singing 'Happy Birthday' that the children love, not the design of the cake! My friend bakes the same cake every year, a Victoria sponge with jam in the middle and icing and Smarties on top. It tastes delicious, looks super-cute and has room for as many candles as you need on top. Most importantly, the whole thing costs her less than a fiver. Bargain!

- Something small to take home. My children sometimes come home from a birthday party with a bag full of sweets and toys that I think must have cost a fortune. We got a party bag once that had a string of fairy lights in it as well as a puzzle, felt tips, a rubber, a toy car…it was ridiculous! Give everyone a slice of cake in a napkin as they leave and they will be delighted. If you want to give them a party bag, keep it small and simple with something cute like a novelty rubber or a yo-yo. It is not your job to keep them in toys for the year!

The Food Shop

How often do you go to the supermarket to pick up a few essentials and come away having spent a fortune?

Remember, supermarkets are there to make money and they know what they are doing! For example, there's a reason they always put the bread in the corner furthest away from the entrance: they want to get you walking past as many products as possible, before you reach the boring old bread…the only thing you came in for. And those special offers they have on display by the front door? They're not always a bargain for you – they are often a sales promotion disguised as a money-saving deal. They put them there because if you see it as soon as you walk in, you're more likely to pick it up, while you're feeling fresh and ready to shop.

Just by thinking that little bit smarter about your supermarket shop, you can shave pounds off your weekly total. Try this next time and see how much you can save:

- Plan your meals and write a shopping list for what you

need. Don't buy anything that isn't on the list and you won't be wasting anything.

- Remember meat and fish are expensive, so try to plan for some vegetarian meals as well.
- Try shopping at the end of the day, when they are marking things down to get them off the shelves.
- Look at the price per 100g, not the item price. You'll notice how much more expensive some things are, but the way they are priced makes it hard to tell.

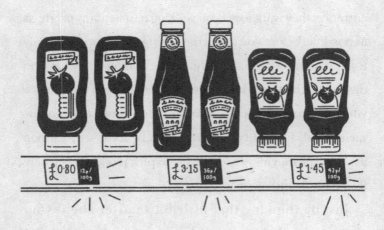

£0·80 12p/100g   £3·15 36p/100g   £1·45 42p/100g

- Buy your fruit and veg loose. They can sometimes cost twice as much simply because they are pre-packaged.

- Buy fruit and veg that are in season. That usually means they've been grown in the UK so they don't come with expensive food miles in the price (and they're better for the environment). If you can't live without your strawberries and summer fruits in December, have a look at some of the frozen options, as these can often still be UK-grown and cheaper than buying things that have been flown in from Africa or Australia.

Top Tip: **Don't shop when you are hungry! You'll want to buy everything. After dinner, when it's quiet and the markdowns are out, is my favourite time.**

Household Bills

No one likes thinking about household bills, that's something we can all agree on. But I am always astonished by people who ignore their bills or who don't shop around when choosing suppliers. It's like going to a fruit and veg market and only buying stuff from the first stall you come to! You wouldn't do that, would you? You'd have a good look around to see who has the juiciest fruit at the best prices. So why throw away money on your electricity or phone bills when all you need to do to make big savings is shop around a little bit more?

I am always astonished by people who ignore their bills or who don't shop around when choosing suppliers. It's like going to a fruit and veg market and only buying stuff from the first stall you come to!

There is so much choice and variation in prices out there that I guarantee you are spending more than you need to on some of these services. All it takes is a little bit of effort and you'll be saving yourself a fortune in no time. Here are a few tips for keeping those pesky bills as low as possible:

Get on it ASAP: As tempting as it is to let the bills and renewal letters pile up in the hall, I always respond to any kind of letter from a supplier as soon as it arrives. Why? Two reasons. Firstly, they will likely be offering you a really good deal in that letter, but the longer you leave it to let them know, the higher their prices will get. Think of it like buying cheap airline tickets: the further in advance you can book, the better the price. The same goes for your electricity and your car insurance and almost every other major household bill. They want to know if you are on board for another 12 months, so they incentivise you with a low price. Secondly, it is so stressful having all these bills and letters staring at you from the sideboard! As someone who suffers from anxiety, I want to get these demands off my to-do list ASAP. It might be a short-term win to block it out and think about it another day, but the long-term effect of letting things like that back up means a bigger headache in the end.

Top Tip: *Even if you can't pay the bill or afford the price they are asking, call them up and deal with it straight away. Most suppliers will want to help you find a way to manage your payments. Ignoring their letters won't help you resolve the issue, so take a deep breath and pick up the phone. You will feel a lot better afterwards for having dealt with it.*

Use price comparison sites: Well-established price comparison websites like Compare The Market and Look After My Bills are worth using. They stay up to date on all the latest offers and schemes across all household bills and services, from insurance and electricity to security and broadband, so you don't have to.

Switch it up: Changing to new energy suppliers for gas and electricity has never been easier. Just go online and use one of the many services now available to help you find the right supplier and the right tariff. These days the switching is all done by the energy providers – you won't need to fill out complicated forms or anything like that – and you will save yourself loads of money. (You can do this even if you rent your home, by the way. If you pay the bills, you are entitled to switch suppliers.)

Take meter readings: It's too easy to just go with whatever the electric or gas estimates are and forget about it. But unless you give them the proper information, you are going to be paying either too much, in which case the energy suppliers will have more of your money than they should, or too little, in which case you're going to be hit with a big bill at some point when they work it all out. It's much easier now to take a meter reading and do it all via your supplier's app. Go and do it now!

Get a water meter: You can't switch your water supplier, as it's water from near where you live. But if you've got more bedrooms than people in your home (lucky you), you might be better off getting a water meter fitted. That way you get more accurate bills based on what you actually consume.

Check for grants: There are loads of grants available for energy-efficient home improvements like new boilers and loft insulation, especially if you receive certain benefits or tax credits. Products are innovating all the time, so keeping things up to date means your bills will be lower and you'll be doing your bit for the environment as well. Search online for boiler and insulation grants, or ask your local council or Citizens Advice branch.

Don't ask; don't get: We have Sky TV and when it was the end of our cancellation period a while back, we phoned them and said we were thinking of leaving unless they could better the price. They reduced our bill by £2 per month instead of the increase of £8 per month *and* upgraded us to Sky Q. Phoning your supplier to see if they can beat their prices is such a quick and simple way to save money. More often than not, they are relying on you being too busy to do it. But tell them you've found a better price elsewhere and see what they say. You will be amazed at what they will do to make sure they don't lose your business.

Cars

When I was 17, my dad said he'd go halves with me on a car, if I could save up for my half. I'll never forget the look on his face when I presented him with the £7,000 I'd saved. He'd been thinking I might put in five hundred quid or so! I'd saved hard for my dream car: a Citroen Saxo, blue with a yellow interior. OMG I loved that car.

Cars are my vice. Maybe it's a status thing? I don't know where it comes from or why, but having a good car is important to me. I feel like I'm doing all right when I've got a decent set of wheels.

But cars are expensive! Not only to buy but to maintain and run. Yet there are ways to cut back on your car-related outgoings, if you are prepared to spend a little time on it. For example, when I buy a car, I don't just go to the nearest garage and see what's on the forecourt. I phone up five or six different garages and tell them what I'm after. It is amazing how different their offerings can be for exactly the same vehicle. And I always make sure I phone places from around the country; the prices in the North can be significantly cheaper than where I live in the Southeast. It might mean a journey to go and collect it, but when there are literally thousands of pounds involved, why wouldn't you? Here are some other car-related tips:

- Don't buy new cars! Unless you have got money to burn. A new car will lose significant value as soon as it leaves the showroom. Second-hand or leased cars are cheaper and it's not difficult these days to find used cars that are in mint condition.

- Leasing your car is a great way to keep your monthly car payments down. Rather than its being a loan to pay for the car which you keep at the end, leasing is like renting it from the dealer. You agree to have it for a certain amount of time and can opt to buy it at the end if you want to keep it. I usually keep mine for a maximum of two years and hand it back before I need to pay the big cost of buying it.

- Ask your dealer if they can throw in any extras for you like a free valet or a complimentary service. You don't lose anything by asking!

- Don't spend unnecessary money on petrol. A quick online search will tell you where to find the cheapest petrol near you. What's the point in spending extra on petrol when you don't have to?

- Shop around for car insurance the same way you would for your household bills. Comparison sites are your friends.

Top Tip: **If you have a partner or another person you share the car with, you can add their name to your policy instead of taking out separate cover.**

DO THIS: When we get a renewal quote in for the home insurance or something like that, Adam will spend a whole morning researching prices. He looks at the price comparison sites, but he also makes calls to check it's the best possible price. You might think that sounds like a lot of effort, but sometimes the savings are hundreds of pounds, and not many of us are making that for a couple of hours' work, are we? Give it a go: put a little time aside to do your research and see how much you can save yourself.

Phones, Tech and Electronics

When I was about 15, I decided I wanted my own TV in my bedroom, and my parents said I'd have to save up for it myself. So I did. It took me about three months of working at the greengrocers but I got there in the end: a £110 TV from Albany Radio, which was a kind of second-hand electronics retailer. You don't see them around so much any more but back then there was one on every high street, and you could buy pretty much anything electronic you needed second-hand from there.

I had a small bedroom – there was room for my single bed and that was about it – so I had the TV at the end of my bed and thought I was in heaven. It was such an achievement, my first 'major' purchase, and I had done it all by myself. I guess that's a feeling that has never left me.

I still like having nice tech, only these days it's a bit more sophisticated than my old square telly with the aerial on top. I've got a laptop, a tablet and a mobile phone. And that's just me. Factor in all of Adam's gadgets, the kids' screens and the TV, and we are practically an electronics retailer ourselves!

There's no getting around the fact that most of us can't get along without our tech these days – if I didn't have a phone, I would never have started posting on Instagram and I wouldn't be here writing this book. I know that without the TV and all the content we access online every day, the Covid-19 pandemic would have been so much more difficult to get through. Put simply, it's pretty much an essential part of life. But that doesn't mean we have to spend a fortune on devices or on service providers. As with everything money-saving, if you can spend a little bit of time on the research you can shave large amounts off your tech bills every month. Here are some suggestions:

- Recycle your old mobile phone. That old handset sitting in the back of your drawer could be worth a couple of hundred pounds or more. There are a number of mobile phone recycling websites, where you can put in your model and see what it might be worth. You pop it in the post and get paid for your old phone! Just remember to set it back to factory settings before you send it.

Top Tip: *If it's a really old phone, it's worth checking on eBay, as some people collect old tech and will pay incredible amounts for something they really want. The older and rarer the model, the better. If you've got one of the first Nokia phones from the 1980s, you could get up to £1,000 for it on eBay!*

- If you're taking out a monthly mobile contract, make sure you set up text alerts for when you are near the end of your data allowance. That way you can watch what you are using and avoid racking up loads of extra charges.
- Beware unlimited this and unlimited that. So many packages offer you endless hours of data or texts but, actually, what do you need? Really think hard about how you use your phone and get a deal that works for you.
- Mobile providers' stores and call centres all have different price plans and options, so shop around. You might find a better price over the phone even if it's the same company as on the high street.

Travelling

We all love getting away, and eating out in new places is definitely one of the best things about being on holiday for me. But something that really bugs me is how expensive everything is in the cafés and restaurants at airports and service stations. They know you are tired and hungry and probably have grumpy kids with you, then they cash in on that by charging outrageous prices, just because they can! We're like sitting ducks.

The way to beat them is simple. Plan ahead. Work out if you're going to be waiting around in departure lounges. If you think you'll get hungry, take sandwiches or snacks with you to eat instead of wasting money at the cafés. Me and Adam love an egg mayonnaise sandwich, so that's what we always take to the airport. It's become a kind of family ritual – we all look forward to it! Take whatever you like from home, and don't forget a big bottle of water and a flask for your tea or coffee. It's a little bit of effort before you go, but it means you have more to spend on ice creams for the kids and the things that really matter when you are away.

Out and about

Egg mayonnaise sandwiches aren't just for airports! Take a packed lunch with you and some water in a reusable bottle whenever you go to the shops or for a day out. The chances are you are already spending quite a bit if you are off to the shops, and if you throw in a family meal with drinks and puddings and everything else, it can become a really expensive experience. Before you know it, you've spent a fortune on a rubbish shopping-centre dinner, and you might as well have gone on holiday! A little forward thinking can take the sting out of things and leave you with extra to put away for that all-important savings goal.

Top Tip: If you've got small children, there's definitely no need to order them their own meals. Use a side plate and chop up a few bits of what you are having. The money you save will serve them a lot better in their Junior ISA than on that plate (which may end up on the floor anyway).

Public transport

This is a no-brainer. Why take the car into town and pay for petrol and parking, when you can catch a bus or a train? Public transport is cheaper and better for the environment. Even cheaper and even better for you is going by foot! Walking to work or wherever you need to go is hands down the best way to build exercise into your day *and* save on petrol money or bus fare. Yes, it takes longer, but if you stick your headphones on and listen to a good audiobook or some music, you'll arrive at your destination feeling like you've had some real me-time. Of course, we all need a car to get to places at times, but if you leave the car at home for just one day a week, you'll make some serious savings without even thinking about it. Here's an example:

TRAVEL TO WORK
- Petrol Cost : £4
- Bus tickets : £2·10
- Walk : Free

Switching 1 day/week would save

	/week	/year
Bus	£1·90	x52 = £98·80
Walk	£4	x52 = £208

DO THIS: Still filling up when you go to the petrol station? You'll get more mileage to the gallon if you keep your tank around half-full. How come? Because you'll be driving around with less weight, and the heavier your car, the more petrol it uses to move. Also take your roof rack off while you're not using it, and make sure you're not driving around with loads of stuff in the boot – it all adds to the weight.

Reward Schemes

Whatever you are buying, the majority of stores offer some kind of reward or loyalty scheme. It's a way of getting you to keep coming back to the same store or brand, by offering you discounts on repeat purchases (the things you buy most often) or getting you to try new products by giving you money off. Some of them give you points to spend like money in the store, while others give you vouchers or free gifts. Even my local brow bar does it – get your brows done nine times and the tenth is free. Like everything money-saving, these schemes are great as long as they work for *you* and not the retailer.

With any shop you buy from regularly, it is always worth getting the app. Most reward schemes are linked to the store app, and often they give you even bigger discounts than just using your card in the shop. Use the app even if you are physically in the store and you'll find you get access to loads of better deals. Stores like knowing what you are spending your money on, so they want you to use the app and will entice you with bigger, better deals.

Avoid over-buying things you don't need just because you've got a discount code or a voucher. Always consider your purchases and apply my Hourly Rate Principle (see page 34), even if the discounts seem too good to pass up. Do you really need eight bags of cotton wool, just because there's a deal on?

Store cards

The older, wilier sister of your reward card, the store card offers you lots of the same attractive discounts but is usually tied in with a credit provider. It is basically a credit card, and you are borrowing money from a financial institution when you use one to pay for something in your favourite shop.

Store cards often offer you discounts and VIP access to sales and other incentives that can seem attractive, but having a store card also makes it easy to buy more than you need, because it gives you the illusion of having limitless cash at your disposal; it's that buy now, pay later mentality that I don't want to encourage!

Most store cards also have really high interest rates and can catch you out if you are not extra careful about making repayments and clearing that balance as soon as you get the bill every month.

You won't usually hear me recommending the use of store cards, apart from when opening one means you get a juicy discount on something you really need, like a new TV or a dishwasher. And then be sure to cancel it as soon as you can.

Other Ways to Get Discounts and Savings

Blue Light Card

If you're a member of the emergency services or armed forces, or you work for the NHS or in the social-care sector, you can get loads of brilliant discounts in all the high street stores with a Blue Light Card. Check out their website (www.bluelightcard.co.uk) for full details.

Honey

This fab little browser extension sits on your search bar and finds all the online discount codes for you. It also lets you earn points and gives you vouchers. I always use it when I buy anything online.

KidStart

This shopping hub puts money in your kids' Junior ISAs every time you buy anything online from most UK major retailers. How cool is that? Sign up and get the little savings prompt extension that will remind you to shop via the KidStart hub.

Annual delivery

ASOS, Amazon, Next and loads of other retailers offer a one-off price for annual delivery. Usually only costing the same as a couple of one-off purchases, it gives you free delivery for the year, and often it's express or 48-hour. This is a rare example of me recommending you actually spend money, but if you are going to be buying from a certain retailer a lot, it is definitely worth doing.

Google Shopping

If you are looking for something quite specific like a certain model of television or a blouse in a particular size and colour, do a quick Google search and then hit the Shopping tab. It will give you links to all the places you can buy the product, along with the prices, so you can see almost instantly where the cheapest place to buy it is.

Newsletters

Newsletters are some of the most effective marketing tools for brands because they can send messages directly to your inbox and include links that take you to their website. In fact, I don't know about you but my inbox seems to be full of messages from companies these days, and hardly any personal emails!

Most companies will offer you a discount code or some other incentive to sign up for their newsletter. I always think it's worth doing because it's not causing any harm or costing you anything, and you can unsubscribe once you've used your discount code, if you don't want to keep receiving the emails.

Part Three

Money looks better in the
bank than on your feet

I grew up in the 1980s, when there were still people who would come to your door selling dishcloths and other household items, or insurance or make-up or whatever it was.

The doorbell was always going with people selling you things. Even the rag-and-bone man was still a thing! They didn't use horse-drawn carts by then, but I can remember men in open flat-bed trucks driving slowly down the street shouting, 'Any old iron!' You could take your scrap metal out to them and they'd buy it off you.

We don't see them much any more, but in some ways we are all rag-and-bone men now. Most of us have sold one or two old things on eBay or Gumtree to raise a few quid. I got the old Christmas tree down from the loft just the other day and sold it on Facebook Marketplace along with all the baubles. It went in five minutes flat and the buyer came round to get it about half an hour later. I got £40 for it – not a fortune, but enough to make me feel like the new one won't be costing us quite so much.

The process of becoming a saver like me might start with cutting back on your spending and making changes to your buying habits, but there is also plenty of money to be made in your own home. Even if you think you haven't got anything much to sell, I guarantee there is a whole pile of stuff sitting

Finding the time to start making money from the resources in front of you can be difficult, especially if you're already busy with a job and family.

at the back of your wardrobe or in your loft that someone, somewhere, will buy from you.

And even if you think you can't do anything special or you don't have time to take on extra work, I'll bet you have a skill or something you can do that can help you generate extra cash. But finding the time to start making money from the resources in front of you can be difficult, especially if you're already busy with a job and family. Keep reading to find out not only how and where to sell for the best prices, but also how to make it work for you, so that this new revenue stream becomes a normal part of your life, and not just for Christmas.

Sell, Sell, Sell

There are so many ways to generate an income from your existing possessions, from selling your old phone to auctioning old clothes on platforms like eBay and Depop. Here are some of the best ways to start generating that second income:

Car boot sale

This is a brilliant way to sell all those small, low-value things you've got sitting in boxes in the garage or the loft – the kids' toys and books, all those old pairs of shoes, the vase your aunty gave you for Christmas that you feel bad getting rid of. Doing a good old car boot sale will help you clear the decks and raise a few quid all at the same time. It might seem like a lot of bother, but if you need some motivation, use my Hourly Rate Principle (see page 34). If you think you're going to bring home more than your hourly rate, and you get to declutter at the same time, what's not to like?

Top Tip: **Keep an eye on the weather and make sure you do the car boot sale when the sun is shining and everyone is out and about. Bank holiday weekends are perfect as you'll have more customers and therefore a greater chance of selling your stuff.**

What is decluttering and how do you do it?

Clutter is anything you're keeping in your house that is getting in the way or doesn't add any extra value to your life. Decluttering is about making space for your life right now, and the things that really matter.

If something is useless but you are holding on to it 'just in case' it comes in handy one day, or if you are storing clothing that hasn't been worn for years on the off-chance you might wear it again, then you are officially suffering from a case of clutter. Clutter can be stressful. All that extra stuff around the place is like a weight around your neck. Even if you can't see it, knowing it is sitting there doing nothing can be a burden you don't need. It can also be a hygiene hazard and even a danger if you let it spill over. It's no wonder there are now so many experts, TV programmes and books dedicated to the art of decluttering.

Decluttering can be a really therapeutic process and will free up not only physical but mental space in your life. It can also raise a few quid if you sell all your old stuff! If you can earn a bit extra selling it on to someone who might use it, then that has to be good news, right?

DO THIS: Work your way through each room one by one, starting in the loft or at the top of your house. Take a moment to look at every item and ask yourself if you're really going to wear that jacket again or read that book, or if you are holding on to it for other reasons. It could be sentimental or because you spent a lot of money on it and think you should get more wear out of it. Whatever it is, if you know in your heart that you're not going to use or wear it again, then put it in the declutter pile and start making some money!

Whatever it is, if you know in your heart that you're not going to use or wear it again, then put it in the declutter pile and start making some money!

Garage sale

These are more popular in the United States, where people often have a big garden and/or a garage, but if you have the space it's worth thinking about holding a garage sale. It means you don't have to cart all your stuff off to the car boot sale, and you don't have to pay a seller's fee. Put posters up and advertise it on your local Facebook groups to let people know you're having the sale. It's perfectly legal to hold a garage sale but just be careful not to make it a regular thing, otherwise the council will see it as a retail market and you might find yourself in trouble.

Top Tip: If you don't have the space, team up with a mate who does, and hold a joint sale. More goodies mean more sales!

---

eBay

I like selling my old clothes and smaller homewares on eBay because I can sell to a nationwide, or even international, audience and get as many people as possible bidding on my items. I also like that when you sell with eBay you are rated by your customers, so it's kind of like building a brand and a loyal customer base. What's more, you're covered legally, and if someone doesn't pay you, you can open up a dispute case and get it sorted.

The things I sell most on eBay have two things in common: they are small enough to post and they come from a good brand that holds its value. Here are some of the things I've sold recently on eBay:

- Designer clothes
- Moncler boy's jacket
- Good-quality shoes (not my old flip-flops)
- Bags, belts and other accessories
- Unused make-up
- Costume jewellery
- Small homewares like candlesticks or placemats

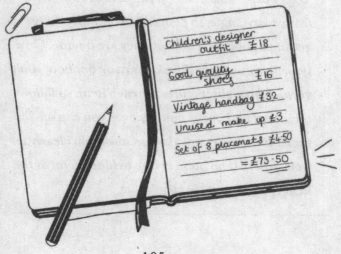

Children's designer outfit £18

Good quality shoes £16

Vintage handbag £32

Unused make up £3

Set of 8 placemats £4·50

= £73·50

How to sell and get the best price: On eBay it's all about the pictures. Find a nice uncluttered space and set up a little home studio with a plain background and some good natural lighting. If it's clothes you're selling, use a wooden hanger, not a plastic one from the supermarket. And, if appropriate, you can add some flowers or a picture frame, just to style it up a bit. Think about the way things look in online shops and try to bring a bit of that style to your images. I get really frustrated when I see someone's messy bedroom in the background or an old mug or something – it puts me right off. With a little effort, you'll see the results in the bids and the prices you achieve.

Top Tip: *Take loads of pictures of your item, from every angle, so people feel they are really getting a good look at what they are buying. On a typical fashion website like Zara or Boohoo, you'll get around eight pictures for each item, so follow their lead and put as many pics as you can on there. If there are any flaws, show them clearly as well – there is no point trying to hide them, as the item will only get sent back!*

Use key words to describe your item: When listing an item, get as many describing words in the title as possible. These 'key' words will make your item more visible when people search for things. Here's an example:

Not the way to do it: Blue top

A better way to do it: Whistles blue silk blouse 12 SS20 vintage fashion

Phone a friend

Not going to lie, selling things on eBay can be time-consuming. So if you find you've got a mounting pile and no time to list it, think about asking someone else to do it and giving them a share of the fee. When everything started taking off for me and being Money Mum became a full-time job, I didn't have enough hours in the day to list all the things I wanted to. So I asked my mate Gemma Lambert (Lambert to me!) to take over selling my stuff. She handles it all and gets a 25 per cent share of everything she sells. She's a busy mum, so she does it whenever she has a minute, and I'm still getting something for all my old bits and pieces. It's a win-win situation for everyone!

Facebook Marketplace

This is a relatively young selling platform and I absolutely love it for shifting larger items at a local level. Brody's old bike, Bronte's old buggy, suitcases, the old dining-room chairs – they have all gone on Facebook Marketplace and sold in a jiffy. Even better, I love that people come and collect their items, so you don't even need to worry about postage and all of that.

As with eBay, you need to take clear photographs and describe your item's faults if there are any, otherwise it'll be coming back home again before you know it!

Top Tip: If I'm selling something in order to replace it with something new, I always try to sell it first so I know what I can spend on the new item. It just helps me avoid any feelings of guilt I might have about a new purchase, when I've got money in my hand from the sale of the old one. Even if you only get a tenner from selling your old crash helmet, that's £10 off the price of the new one. And occasionally you can get lucky and sell the item for more than the price of the one you are buying! I sold some babygros that Bronte had grown out of for £13 and I'd only paid £12 for them new!

Remember: there are lots more selling platforms to consider using. From Depop and Vinted to Gumtree and Shpock, they all have their strengths and weaknesses and they are all aimed at different target markets and users. For example, Depop is really popular with young people selling streetwear and vintage fashion. It might not be the best place to get rid of your old travel cot, but if you've got some cool 1980s roller skates to flog, you're in! Take a moment to look at all the different platforms and really think about where the best place to sell your gear is. It could make a big difference to the sale price.

Turning Assets into Revenue Streams

It's not only clothes and old bits of furniture you can turn into cash. Your home and plenty of other assets can be turned into revenue streams if you think smart about it.

Rent out your spare bedroom

Any landlord knows that renting out a property by the room generates a greater yield (the return on your investment over a period of time) than letting the place as a whole. There's lots of complicated details about why this is, but basically it's because they can charge more rent when it's broken up into individual rooms and can often avoid expensive letting-agency fees.

If you're lucky enough to have a spare room – maybe an older child has left home or you just have the extra space – and you're looking to generate some extra income, renting out your room could be just the ticket. Room rental prices vary according to where you are in the UK but can be anywhere from £500 to £900 a month. Not bad for an empty room you're not using! Look at how much extra money you could earn in a year just by letting that space if you charged £600 a month:

£600 x 12 = £7,200

Obviously it can be a big step having someone new in your house, so always use an accredited service like Spareroom.co.uk who will guide you through the process and make sure everything and everyone checks out.

I used to let my spare room to trainee teachers from France who were doing work experience at my local secondary school. They were all absolutely amazing and I really enjoyed having them at home for what was usually one school term. If you don't want to let out a room full time, you could offer digs to touring performers or language students who are visiting your area for short periods (and probably won't be at home much.) Call up your local theatres, schools and language schools to find out how to get on their accommodation lists.

Rent out your driveway or garage

Here's another nice, easy way to make the most of space you're not using: let your driveway or garage to a commuter. Parking is notoriously difficult and expensive, so people who drive to work, or those who drive to the station and catch the train, are always looking for cheaper places to leave their cars during the day. If you've got space for another car on a drive or in a garage, why not let it out? It will make no difference to you (and can be a burglar deterrent if you're not at home, because it looks like someone is in) and you can earn around £50 a month for one space. It's best to use a specialist app like JustPark, as you don't need to worry about any of the admin – the cash just lands in your account.

Look how much that could make you in a year:

£50 x 12 = £600

That's Christmas paid for!

Top Tip: **Renting a parking space works both ways. If you drive to work or to a specific destination on a regular basis, check out your options for renting a parking space instead of paying extortionate parking fees.**

Rent out your clothes

The clothes rental trend (see page 53) also offers a possible revenue stream. If you've got a special designer dress sitting in your wardrobe or your other half has a gorgeous suit he never wears, you can rent it out and have it make money for you! There are a number of apps now offering clothes rental services. Be sure to check the small print about what happens if items get damaged or lost, and always read your customers' descriptions and reviews if they are available.

Top Tip: **Stay seasonal. There's no point in listing your big winter coat in July or offering a sundress at Christmas. Follow the shops' lead and be a few weeks ahead of the weather, when people are really starting to make plans for the summer or winter.**

Rent out your car

If your car is sitting on the drive all day while you're at work, or maybe you are regularly away at weekends and the car gets left at home, you could try renting it out. The idea of 'peer-to-peer' car sharing is still quite new but like Airbnb or

JustPark, it's about cutting out the middle man and making money from what you've already got. Obviously you need to be OK with strangers using your car, and you probably need to have one that's in decent nick, otherwise nobody will want to hire it! But if you can make it work, the money you earn (up to £650 a month) will pay for all your car-related expenses and some more! There are all sorts of ways to make it easy, with keyless technology and built-in insurance cover. Have a search online and see if it's something you could do.

Rent out your home

Whether you do it via Airbnb or another holiday-letting service, you can make money by letting out your home to other people. Obviously this comes with a few complications – you need to find somewhere else to stay, for starters! And if you live by the sea in Brighton you might have more interest in your home than if you live by an industrial estate off the M1. There's also the issue of having strangers staying in your house, and what to do with all your stuff. Basically, it's not for everyone! But if you can make it work for you, letting your home on Airbnb or similar can bring in some really good money. In 2020 the average rent for a seven-night stay in the UK was around £600! That's £2,400 a month!

Some people I know let their house only when they go on holiday, so their holiday is basically being paid for. Someone else I know lets her flat out one week a month (she goes and stays with her mum) and the money she gets pays the mortgage. Even if you don't live in a 'holiday' area, there are loads of reasons why people might need accommodation, be it travelling for business or visiting relatives. Do your research and work out if it you can realistically make it work for you. If you've got a messy home, or family members who don't like the idea of shipping out on a regular basis, it might not be for you. But if you're a minimalist who likes to get away and you have lots of places where you could stay for a night or two, then it could be a lifesaver.

As with eBay and other peer-to-peer selling platforms, you will live and die by your photos when trying to let your property. Take shots that show all the things you would like if you were staying there – the kitchen looking clean, freshly made beds, nice views if you have them, a comfy living space. Just a little bit of effort before you upload those photos can make a big difference to your bookings.

Gemma's Make Money Day

I know that finding the time and motivation to sell your unwanted items can be hard. The things-to-sell pile grows and grows until eventually you feel overwhelmed just looking at it and it all goes in a bin bag and off to the charity shop or tip. That's why I invented my Make Money Day! It's just a bit of fun and a challenge to set yourself. All you do is choose a day of the week and list *five* items to sell. It could be on eBay or Gumtree or Facebook – there are loads of apps now for specific things like vintage clothes.

You might put up a sign in your newsagent's or in a local newspaper. Just get five things out there on any platform of your choosing and do it every week. You will be amazed at how the extra money coming in builds up.

Top Tip: **If you use PayPal, keep all your earnings in your PayPal account and pay for any postage and packaging out of it as well. That way it feels like a real pot of gold that has nothing to do with your regular bank accounts, and you can see exactly how much you are bringing in from selling your stuff.**

Shape public opinion

No, I don't mean be a politician! But you can take part in online surveys and earn a bit of extra cash. Just go online and search for online survey sites. They all have a slightly different approach, but as a rule you take part in surveys and they pay you either with vouchers or with cash-outs direct to your account. Doing surveys isn't going to make you rich in a hurry, but it can boost your bank balance and is usually something you can do while watching TV – bonus!

Put in the Hours

If you really are on a mission to make some extra money – maybe you need to pay off a debt or you want to accelerate your savings effort – taking on some extra work is going to be a big help.

Obviously if you've already got a job and/or a family, this isn't going to be easy. We are only human and need time to have a life and get some rest occasionally. I am not recommending that anyone runs themselves into the ground or reaches burnout here. But there are plenty of ways you can earn little extra bits here and there, sometimes without even leaving the house.

When I was 14 I got myself a job as a mushroom picker. I know, glamorous! The pay was based on how many mushrooms you picked (by weight) and you could do as much or as little as you wanted. I decided I could get up an hour earlier every day and do an hour at the mushroom farm on my way to school. And that's what I did. It wasn't loads of money – sometimes just £4 or £5 a day – but it was a little bit extra every day and it was something I could bolt onto what I was already doing (going to school!).

What is the gig economy?

Have you heard of the gig economy? Basically it's the name for the way lots of people work nowadays, be it as self-employed freelancers or as regular 'workers' who don't have a contract with an employer but get paid for the 'gigs' they do. Uber drivers are a common example of people working in the gig economy. There has been a lot of controversy about it, because some people think it's exploitative and it means you don't get any job security, holidays, sick pay or any of the other benefits that usually come with having a proper job contract. But the upside of the gig economy is its flexibility. As a delivery driver or a cleaner or whatever you decide to do, you can determine your own hours and earn as little or as much as you want. This makes working in the gig economy rather handy for people who want a second income (aka a side hustle) or need to fit their work around a busy family life or other commitments.

Some of the things you could do for your side hustle:

- Delivery driver
- Taxi/Uber driver
- Cleaner
- Deliveroo/Just Eat rider
- Courier
- Taking in ironing
- Walking other people's dogs
- Babysitting
- Fruit-picking

The great thing about this kind of casual work is that you can do more or less of it depending on your own schedule and things like the time of year. For example, Christmas is always going to be a busy time for delivery drivers as loads of people are ordering things online around then. Summer would be a good time to look into outdoor work like fruit-picking or dog-walking.

Look at what earning just an extra £50 a week will bring in over the year:

£50 x 52 weeks = £2,600

That could pay off a credit card or an overdraft, or pay for an amazing holiday, or go into your savings account to add to your nest egg.

Feeling positive about your money, getting on top of debt, being in charge? That's priceless.

The point is, you don't need to have a big list of qualifications to start pulling in extra cash and really making a difference. And feeling positive about your money, getting on top of debt, being in charge? That's priceless.

So you want to be a mumpreneur?

One of the things that shocked me most about having children was how little time I had all of a sudden! I knew babies would keep me busy, but nothing can really prepare you for how time-consuming and tiring being a mum can be. The thought of going back into a nine-to-five job just seemed impossible. I didn't want to leave my kids at home while someone else looked after them, and what's more, on some days I couldn't get out of my pyjamas!

I had heard about being a mumpreneur and, of course, I knew about women who had made a career while also being a mum, but I had not given it a lot of thought. However, as I got into the groove of being at home with the kids, I began to think about it more and more. I realised it wasn't that I didn't have time or ideas or the drive to want to do something. I just needed it to be something that fitted in around the children, that I could do when they slept or while I was still in my pyjamas. Eventually I set up BB Lingerie with a friend. We felt there was a gap in the market for affordable wedding lingerie (and funnily enough, nice pyjamas) so we went for it, and although being Money Mum is what keeps me busiest of all now, BB is still going from strength to strength.

So many of the mums I followed (still do) on Instagram are women like me, who are talented, have great ideas and want to get on in the world, but also have limited time and resources while their children are at home. Often they've just got a phone or a laptop and that's it! I am so inspired by all the women I see every day working their Instagram accounts to promote their brands, setting up their own websites while the kids are in bed, baking amazing brownies, doing incredible balloons and coming up with all sorts of weird and wonderful things! There are so many of us out there now. It makes me proud to be a woman and a mum and part of that tribe.

Of course, it's not easy if you're a mum with young children – you're going to be tired and emotionally drained, with eight hundred things to do every day and the CBeebies theme on repeat in your head. But if you're thinking about giving your own business a go, here are some tips:

- Do your research and make sure what you're offering is unique.

- Think about what you are good at. There's no point setting up a sandwich delivery if you're a rubbish chef!

- Consider setting up with a friend. It can get lonely doing it by yourself, and another pair of hands, and someone to bounce ideas off, is always useful.

- Believe in what you are doing. I couldn't be Money Mum without really being passionate about saving money.

- Even if you don't set up a business with them, try to find time to hang out with other mumpreneurs and share your tips and advice. I always say that lifting someone else up won't bring you down. If you can help someone one day, they might be able to help you another day. It's all good.

- If you're not sure what you want to do, start small. Try selling a few things on eBay (see page 104) or helping out a friend for a few hours a week. See what you can handle and what feels right for you. Sometimes if things aren't clear it can help just to get going with something – anything – and then the way will become clear.

- Use all the free help that is out there. Organisations like The Prince's Trust and Women in Business have got loads of great advice and resources to help young people and women get on.

- Be kind to yourself and remember that Rome wasn't built in a day.

Part Four

Stop buying things you
don't need, to impress
people you don't like

As you probably know by now, my attitude to money has been pretty much the same ever since I can remember. I was born saving and I'm allergic to debt.

But I know I'm unusual. According to The Money Charity, the average unsecured debt (i.e., not a mortgage) per adult in the UK is now almost £10,000. The average British student leaves university with around £40,000 of debt to pay back. The average credit card debt is around £2,000, and among young people it's much higher. There is just so much temptation out there, you can get almost anything on finance. It's no wonder so many people end up in debt.

When everyone around you is borrowing money and buying things they can't afford, it's hard to be different. It's hard to pass up nice things when out for dinner with friends or on holiday. It's hard to say out loud that you can't afford a new coat or to buy a friend a birthday present. I see it all the time, people pretending they are richer than they are. I get daily messages from people – men and women – who say they can't tell their partners about their spending or they feel out of their depth with borrowing. And I come across people in denial, lying to themselves, who say they can't afford the food shop but then spend a fortune on cosmetic surgery or a new watch. We live in a culture that presents debt to us as

*When everyone around you
is borrowing money and buying
things they can't afford, it's hard
to be different.*

though it's normal. So, I know I can sit here and give you all
the money-saving tips in the world, but if you're surrounded
by people borrowing more and more to buy a lifestyle they
can't afford, it's going to be difficult. I get it. This is where
your money mindset comes in!

Identify your Money Mindset

Never heard of your money mindset? Well, as you'd expect, it is about the way you perceive yourself and your money and the way it affects your behaviour – the way you spend, save, borrow and generally manage your finances. Once you get a handle on this, it starts opening all sorts of doors in your mind that you didn't even know were there.

Reflect

Take some time to think about the kind of money environment you grew up in and how that might have affected your expectations and habits around money. Awareness is everything and understanding why you might be the way you are with money is the first and biggest step towards making the changes you need to make. For example, I know that my parents not giving me extra pocket money when I ran out had a big impact on me. Have a think about how you were raised to interact with money, any big moments you remember, what being 'rich' meant to you as a child and what it means now. It's a really interesting thing to do! Writing it down, or 'journalling', always helps.

What is journalling?

Journalling is a really useful tool if you are thinking about change or asking some big questions about yourself and your life, which is why I think it's so helpful when you are reflecting on your money mindset. There are no rules, you just write down what comes into your head. It could be that you never had any money as a kid, or you feel worried that you won't ever get on the property ladder. It could even be admitting that you enjoy spending money. Whatever it is, by writing it all down in a journal you usually find some answers to those big questions you are asking yourself. My favourite thing about journalling? It's practically cost-free – all you need is a pen and notebook and you are off.

Top Tip: Experts say our minds are at their most 'free' first thing in the morning, so try writing something as soon as you get up, before the day starts closing in on you. You might be surprised at what you end up writing!

Learn your zones

Psychologists at Sheffield University have worked out that there are four main human behaviour zones when it comes to money:

- The **comfort zone** is where you are stuck in a familiar rut, not doing anything to change your habits or move your finances forward.

- The **fear zone** is where you step out of the comfort zone and acknowledge that you need to make some changes if you want things to move forward financially. It's called the fear zone because just admitting that you're going to have to do something is scary! But if you can get a grip in this zone, things will start to get really interesting!

- The **learning zone** is where you start to make a plan of action, to decide where and what you are going to. You begin to gather knowledge about your options and use that knowledge to make plans that will help you grow.

- The **growth zone** is where you start to take action. You might be researching the best deals or making a spreadsheet, or doing a No Spend Day (see page 42). This zone is where you start to take control and manage your finances.

Knowing what zone you are in, and recognising your behaviour around money while you are in it, is a really revealing exercise that will help you identify your money mindset. It's a bit like looking in the mirror and catching yourself from an angle you've never seen before. Remember, you can move through the zones at any time, and some situations may put you in different zones at the same time. It's not a rigid framework, but just a useful way to see yourself and where you are at on your financial journey.

DO THIS: Write down what zone you think you are in now and why. Then write down what zone you would like to be in and what you need to do to get there. Even just scribbling it down on a piece of paper is a big step towards becoming more aware of your financial situation and making the changes you need to make.

Want or need?

As well as working out your money mindset, there are plenty of other ways to adapt your behaviour around money and start making changes at a mental and emotional level. One of the simplest and most useful tools in my money mindset bag is my little Want or Need Test.

It's a bit like the decluttering exercise where you ask yourself if you really, truly love something or if you are holding on to it for vague reasons or out of fear. This simple, four-question quiz will help you in those moments when you're not sure whether to buy something or not.

Crucial questions

Next time you are about to spend money on something that you're not sure you should be spending it on, ask yourself these four questions:

1. Is this necessary for my family's (including my own) health or safety?
2. Is it vital for something else?
3. Can I wait a while before I have to buy it?
4. Have I got any acceptable alternatives?

1. Is this necessary for my family's (including my own) health or safety?

   No!

2. Is it vital for something else?

   Erm, no.

3. Can I wait a while before I have to buy it?

   Of course!

4. Have I got any acceptable alternatives?

   I'm pretty sure you've got some shoes!!

If your answers to all four questions are like these, it means you definitely don't need the shoes. You just want them.

Now don't get me wrong, it's OK to want things – I want things all the time. But knowing that you only want them and don't need them can be a good way to help you decide whether to spend the money or not.

Tip: Use my Hourly Rate Principle (see page 34) to ask yourself if the want is worth the work you have to put in to pay for these shoes. Quite often you will find it's not.

Sitting with your feelings

If you have ever tried mindfulness or read any psychology magazines, you might have come across the phrase 'sit with your feelings'. But what does it mean and how does it apply to saving money?

Sitting with your feelings is basically about recognising when you feel something uncomfortable;

it could be anything from feeling embarrassed or shy to being angry or just plain old sad. Whatever your uncomfortable feelings are, the idea that you 'sit' with them is about accepting them and not trying to fight them or react to them in any way. You just notice them and sit with them until they pass – because most of our feelings are temporary, especially the uncomfortable ones.

Sitting with your feelings is a great skill to nurture for loads of situations in life, but it is especially helpful when you are struggling with a want-or-need situation, or with other negative emotions linked to money. Maybe you are desperate to have an item of clothing at any cost, or you feel like a failure because you can't afford something. Maybe you're angry at yourself for overspending, or are bewildered or overwhelmed by the scale of your debts.

It can be tempting to get rid of these uncomfortable feelings by going out and splashing your cash or buying all the drinks, 'treating' yourself to things you don't need and generally doing the opposite of what is helpful in the long run.

Next time you feel uncomfortable about money, try just sitting with it. Notice how you feel. Maybe it affects you in a physical way – you might clench your jaw, grind your teeth or feel a bit tight in your stomach. Whatever it is, instead of hitting the buy button or maxing out your credit card, just sit with it. Write it down in your journal if it helps. Let the feeling pass through you. You might find it passes sooner than you expect, and you come out of the other side feeling stronger and more confident about who is in control when it comes to your money mindset. (Clue: it's you!)

When Shopping Becomes a Problem

The reasons behind our shopping urges

You know by now that I always enjoy a bit of shopping! Let's face it, most of us like a little splurge down the shops, whether it is online or on the real high street. For a lot of people, that means buying new clothes, but for others it can be anything from vintage watches or make-up to plants or tropical fish. But *why* do we enjoy shopping so much? What is it about the thrill of handing over cash and getting new things that keeps us coming back for more?

The scarcity impulse

It is part of our basic, human nature to gather around us things that please us and make us feel happy and secure. In fact, psychologists have labelled this the 'scarcity impulse'.

It comes from our hunter-gatherer days when, if we saw something that might be useful, like a fistful of berries or a delicious-looking animal, we would grab it even if we didn't need it at that moment. It is basically a survival instinct, like hauling stuff back to our cave in case we need it sometime. I love that idea!

Obviously, scarcity isn't a major problem for most of us these days, but the instinct to grab things while we can is still there, and shops are very clever at marketing products to us in ways that tap into our scarcity impulse. All those buy-one-get-one-free deals and end-of-season half-price sales are

designed to trigger the thought, somewhere deep inside your brain, that if you don't snap up this product now, you might live to regret it.

Retail therapy

Another reason why so many of us like a spot of shopping is that it makes us feel in control. If we are feeling fed up or stressed or like nothing is going our way, buying something gives us a sense of power. It says we are the one making the choices here – we are calling the shots. That's why it's called retail therapy! It is literally activating the reward system in our brain that makes us feel good.

Building our own brand

And, of course, now that we have social media, the choices we make about the way we look and the way we live have never seemed so important as they do now. Shopping is a way of defining ourselves, of telling people who we are. We attach ourselves to certain brands and materials and items, in order to build our own brand. There's a good reason you won't see me posting pictures on Instagram of myself wearing high-priced clothes and shopping at the expensive supermarkets – because I'm Money Mum! And I'm all about saving money. But if I was an influencer who was all about luxury or sport or whatever, I might be posting more pictures of me wearing luxury brands and crazy-price trainers. It's mad when you start to think about it.

Spiralling out of control

All of these things are pretty harmless for most people. But for some of us the urge to buy things, whatever is driving it, can get out of hand and become an addiction. If circumstances mean you are feeling out of control more often than not, buying something can become a way of trying to fix your problem, even if only for a moment. The urge to gather and hoard can become overwhelming and you can't stop yourself from buying things you don't need. You begin to feel that you can't be seen without the 'right' clothes or decor or whatever it is you think defines you.

These habits can very quickly spiral and become addictions. And like a lot of addictions, spending can begin to damage your life if you don't get help to fix it. I hear from so many people who have lost their relationships, got into problem debt, had to sell their homes, all because they just couldn't stop spending.

How do you know if your spending habit is an addiction?

Like other addictions, spending is something that the addicted person physically needs to do. They actually crave making a transaction and they get itchy and restless when they can't spend money.

There are loads of different kinds of spending addictions. It might be that someone likes collecting things such as shoes or bags, and they just need to have as many of one particular kind of product as possible. Or it could be only buying really expensive items to show off and feel powerful on social media. There is even what's called 'spending bulimia', which is when you develop a habit of buying loads of things and then taking them all back.

Questions to ask yourself

There's no official way to diagnose a spending addiction, but you can ask yourself questions such as the following and get a pretty good idea of whether your habits are becoming problematic:

- Are you hiding your purchases from your partner because you feel ashamed?
- Are you are buying endless versions of the same thing and hoarding them?

- Are you agitated when you haven't bought anything for a while?
- Do you feel like you have to have something, even if you can't afford it?
- Do you feel low or depressed about your relationship with shopping?
- Are you having trouble sleeping because you are thinking about what and how to buy?

Hiding the evidence

Another possible indication that you might be developing a spending addiction is when you find yourself trying to hide the evidence of your purchases. Have you done any of the following?

- Clearing your browsing history online so that no one else can see what you are buying
- Having items delivered to work or another address so that your partner or family doesn't know you've bought things
- Taking control of jobs like recycling so you can hide the packaging
- Secretly doing online banking so your partner doesn't get the full picture

Whatever your spending habits, if it feels like your need to buy things is becoming a problem, ask yourself honestly what you would say to a friend in the same position. Would you tell them not to worry, or would you suggest they seek help? That's your answer.

Why is a spending addiction a problem?

You might think being addicted to spending money isn't such a bad addiction to have. It's not a physically harmful substance like drugs or alcohol, it doesn't hurt anyone, it makes you feel happy. Right? Well, yes, but it's not that simple. Unlike most other addictions, where you have to pay for your fix up front, you can walk into your favourite store at

If you think your spending is becoming an addiction, first of all remember there is nothing to be ashamed of.

any time and if you haven't got the money you need to spend there and then, they will give you a store card to help you fuel your addiction. You can get loans from the bank and pay-in-three deals online to pay for almost anything these days. It's an addiction that is actively encouraged by shops and lenders. And if your problem buying gets out of hand, you can quickly find yourself in debt – which is the exact opposite of where you want you to be!

If you think your spending is becoming an addiction, first of all remember there is nothing to be ashamed of. I don't know many people who aren't affected by some kind of addiction at some point, and spending is an easy one to fall victim to. Secondly, as with other addictions, there is loads of help and support out there for people who are struggling. You do not have to fix this alone. Contact details for organisations that can help are on page 168. But maybe it's as simple as talking to a friend or a family member first. The hardest thing to do is admit you need help. Do that and everything else will fall into place.

Social Media: It's Complicated

When it was my 40th birthday in 2021, my mum and dad both really spoiled me with jewellery and perfume from one of my favourite designers. When I shared my gifts on Instagram, a few people expressed surprise that I was 'showing off' my fancy things, especially as I'm Money Mum and I'm meant to be all about saving money. This made me so sad! Why can't we be pleased for other people when we see them doing well?

I really believe that as a society we don't talk enough about the good feelings that come with having a bit of financial security and the sense of strength and personal growth that comes with saving and saving up. We talk about being rich or poor, but not about feeling safe or secure, proud or free, or just excited to be alive and being spoiled for your birthday! All of these things come with financial security. But for some reason, we don't celebrate it when someone is doing well.

It doesn't help that social media isn't always a friendly place. I've forged a whole career based on the platform Instagram has given me, and I've made some real friends for life through being on it. I'm constantly amazed at how you can connect with people from all over the world, and I can't believe all the incredible people I've met and chatted to online. I can honestly say it has changed my life.

But it also has a dark side. I've been shocked by the way people I've never met have behaved towards me on social media. I don't like to give them oxygen by repeating the things they've said, but there have been some really nasty comments online, from people who obviously don't like seeing me doing well. Saying I'm a liar, mocking my spelling and grammar because I'm dyslexic, and saying really unkind things about my children.

Obviously, this kind of interaction makes anyone feel upset and anxious. It's horrible to be on the receiving end of stuff like that. And you don't need to be in the public eye to experience it. The free and open nature of the way social media works means that while nine out of ten people will use it for good reasons, there will always be someone who takes advantage of it to spread hate and negativity. So even though I have gained so much from social media, I do also feel very conflicted about it and the effects it can have on us all. Being

We talk about being rich or poor, but not about feeling safe or secure, proud or free, or just excited to be alive and being spoiled for your birthday!

an anxious person, I worry a lot, so knowing that there are people out there saying those things can really knock my confidence and self-esteem some days.

Even without nasty messages, just seeing other people's perfect lives and comparing yourself with them can be enough to make you feel low. I do it all the time! I'm lucky because Adam usually gives me a reality check and we have a bit of a laugh about it. But without him to keep me on the straight and narrow, I know I'd be even worse about comparing myself with other people and their Insta-perfect lives.

My number one piece of advice, if you're ever feeling overwhelmed by social media, is to take a break. Just switch off and get out and do something else. The world is still turning, and after a while away from it all, the problems you think you've got don't always seem so big.

I also suggest you block anyone who makes you feel negative or uncomfortable. Do not engage in conversations with people who want to bring you down. If you don't want to block them completely, you can hide them or mute them. There are loads of ways to remove yourself from conversations you don't want to be in.

Don't Google yourself, either. It is the equivalent of asking someone you have never met and who doesn't know you to tell you what they think of you. Would you do that in real life? No! So don't do it online. You can't control what other people think of you. If they want to be negative and judge you, that's on them. Focus on yourself, how you feel about yourself and building that up.

And finally, I always say: spread the love. Like people's posts, share their good news, send congratulations and hearts and party emojis all over the internet! Give people a whoop-whoop and cheer them on. I always try to share the accounts of people who get in touch or who need a boost. Why wouldn't I? We need to change the conversation and celebrate it when we see other people looking after themselves and making things happen. Good vibes are free, and they never sell out.

Let's Talk About Debt

It would be a bit unrealistic of me to write a book about saving without talking about debt. And the first thing I want to say is: *If you are in debt, don't panic!* You are not alone. Almost everyone is in some kind of debt these days. A mortgage is basically a big debt. If you've got a credit card or a loan of any kind, you've got debt. We can all access credit so easily that we can get into debt in a few clicks on the phone. Debt is very good at getting everywhere.

But it is also very good at getting out of control quickly. Monthly payments here and there all add up, and unless you are really disciplined about staying on top of them, it can be easy to miss payments and find yourself in a mess. There are also a lot of unscrupulous companies that target people who are already in debt and facing financial difficulties, and then offer them easy-to-get credit cards with insanely high interest rates, or payday loans. Known as 'subprime lenders', these companies make out they are there to help by 'consolidating' or paying off your existing debts, but often will land you in more hot water than before. It's not difficult to see how debts can quickly accumulate and become really difficult to manage. Let me tell you, it is my worst nightmare!

Debt and mental health

This kind of problem debt takes its toll on our mental health. Being chased by creditors, feeling you can never get on top of it all, keeping secrets from family and friends – these are all heavy emotional burdens to carry. They can cause relationship breakdowns, serious anxiety and other mental health problems if they are left untended. It works the other way around as well. People with existing mental health problems like bipolar disorder or depression can be prone to overspending, problem gambling and lack of control around money and credit. It's a toxic relationship none of us needs to be in. In 2010 a study by the Royal College of Psychiatrists revealed that half of UK adults living with problem debts also experienced mental health issues including lack of sleep, anxiety, low mood and more serious mental health disorders.

The second thing I want to say about problem debt is: *We can fix it.* I am always so saddened when I hear from people who are struggling and who think there's nothing they can do about it. Feeling hopeless is just the worst feeling, and

I am here to tell you that there is no amount of debt that isn't fixable, somehow.

When debt feels overwhelming

In January 2021, Mick Norcross, star of the reality TV show *The Only Way Is Essex*, took his own life. He'd been facing financial problems and had recently taken out massive loans against his family home to pay for property developments that had been held up by the pandemic. He'd apparently told a friend that the money wasn't worth the 'agg' (aggravation) and he'd be better off topping himself. Two years earlier, another reality show star from Essex, Mike Thalassitis, had taken his own life, also facing spiralling debts. Mike, who'd appeared on *Love Island*, had reportedly overextended himself with a party lifestyle that did not match his earnings, and he felt he had no way out.

I'd known for a long time that there was a link between suicide and debt. But these two men, who'd grown up near me and spent their lives on the same turf as me, and who both seemed to the outside world as if they were doing so well in life, brought home the stark reality of how debt can have terrible consequences.

In 2018, Britain's National Health Service commissioned an Adult Psychiatric Morbidity Survey, which made for some pretty sad reading. It found that people who were in problem debt are *three* times more likely to consider taking their own life, that over 420,000 people in problem debt had considered taking their own life in England the previous year and that 100,000 had actually attempted it. That's right: 100,000 people had tried to end their lives because they owed money and couldn't see a way out of their debt.

It makes me so sad that in one of the world's most advanced economies, people are taking their own lives because of debt. Death by suicide related to debt is a tragedy that affects so many people, and one that can be avoided. I'm not saying it's easy or that you can click your fingers and simply get rid of the debt. And I know just how crippling that sense of failure and shame can be, especially for those of us who feel it's our duty to provide for our families. But believe me when I say that there are many, many other options and organisations who can help you, not only to get out of debt but also to rebuild your sense of self-worth and purpose.

Some useful sources of information and help are given on page 168, but if you are worried about debt, your local Citizens Advice branch and the StepChange Debt Charity are the best places to start. The people there are so understanding and will not judge you, no matter how bad you think your debt is. Make that first leap of faith and see how things start to immediately feel better.

How to avoid being in debt

I can't fix all your problems here, but let me just talk you through a few basic principles in relation to debt and getting out of it. Everyone's circumstances are different, and you can owe £500 and feel mega-stressed about it or £500,000 and not bat an eyelid! But whatever your debt situation, if you are trying to save and make money there are three rules you need to follow:

Rule no. 1: Pay off your debts before trying to save

There is simply no point in trying to save money while you are paying off a debt (other than a mortgage, which is what's called a secured debt and which means you end up with a house at the end of it all).

Why? Because the interest you earn on any savings you make is almost always lower than the interest you pay on your credit card or loan (unless you have discovered the only savings account in the land with a 40 per cent interest rate!). So the debt will always be costing you more than you are earning on the savings. And the longer your debt's shelf life, the more it will cost you overall. If you have a savings account and a credit card with the same bank, you might as well be writing them cheques every month, because of the amount of money they'll be making from you. You are basically lending them money (your savings), for which they are paying you a very low rate of interest, and then they are charging you to borrow it back (your debt) at a much higher rate of interest! It is bonkers.

Example: You have a loan of £5k, which at 5 per cent costs £250 a year. £5k savings in a bank account paying 1 per cent earns you £50 a year. So if you are saving while also paying off the loan, you are actually £200 worse off than if you just paid off the loan.

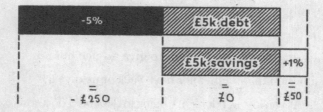

The only time it is worth saving while you still also have debt is if that debt is interest-free, so that the amount of interest your savings are earning is making you more than the debt is costing you. If you can save and keep the debt without it costing you anything, and you are happy keeping the debt, then saving your money is worth doing.

Student loans

Student loans are complicated! I didn't go to university and I can't imagine what it must be like for young people to graduate with all that debt. Still, I'm not here to talk politics. The fact is that today the average student leaves university with around £40,000 to pay back to the Student Loans Company. Rightly or wrongly, governments can change the interest rates on these loans as well as the terms and conditions and all sorts. So I'm reluctant to give advice here on a situation that might alter next week or next year.

As you know, I don't like being in debt but I do know that student loans are some of the cheapest and best-value loans available. And generally speaking, you only need to start paying them back when you earn above a certain threshold. So while I would usually advise you to pay off your debts in the shortest amount of time possible, with student loans it might be that making the minimum payments, or even taking a payment holiday if you need to, is actually a sensible option.

The main thing with a student loan is to make sure you do your research. I hear lots of stories about people overpaying when they don't need to, and not understanding confusing loan statements. If you aren't sure about something, call up the Student Loans Company (find contact details at: www.gov.uk/guidance/guidance-on-contacting-the-student-loans-company) and speak to a real adviser there who will help you understand your options.

Rule no. 2: Pay off the debts with the highest rates of interest first

Why? Because they are the debts costing you the most! It's so easy to make monthly payments and not think about it, because you haven't got anything physical to show for them. They are just numbers on your bank statement. But try imagining your debt repayments as items you are shopping for in the supermarket: look at the price, compare, get the cheapest deal.

Rule no. 3: Transfer your loans and credit card balances to cheaper deals

This is another thing you absolutely need to do. Every loan is different and you will have to check your terms and conditions regarding transfers, but it is so worth doing! It might seem boring, like shopping for insurance, but it will only take an hour of your time and could save you hundreds of pounds – and not many of us are earning that kind of money by the hour, right?

It's basically switching your credit card debt over to a new provider who offers you zero per cent interest if you move to them. However, that rate is usually only for a limited time, so you absolutely must stay aware of when the zero per cent interest period is up. At that point, you either move again or, ideally, will have paid off your balance before the time is up! Have a search online for zero per cent balance transfer cards and see which providers are offering the best deals.

Top Tip: *Paying off a debt doesn't usually have the same thrill factor as buying something new, but that's because there's not anything physical to show for it – no nice bag or shiny packaging comes with closing that credit card down. But what paying off a debt lacks in visibility, it more than makes up for in the sense of freedom and relief you gain. Paying off debt is a massive weight off your shoulders, so celebrate it! Run yourself a lovely bath and put some gorgeous wax melts on, listen to some great music, watch a favourite film, go for a walk with a mate, do whatever makes you feel good. You don't even need to tell anyone else about it, just make sure you are acknowledging this release to yourself, and enjoy walking that little bit taller.*

DO THIS: Write down in your journal some of the free things you can do to celebrate your freedom from debt, and tick them off every time you make a payment or get rid of an outstanding balance. For me it would always be a pamper night with a face mask and maybe doing my nails – just a bit of time to look after myself. What will you do?

Talk to the experts

If you are really struggling with your debts and you think you can't find a way through, there are a number of organisations and services that can come to your aid. Please don't be afraid to ask for help – it is a sign of strength, not weakness. Money and debt can be complicated and there are experts who can help you find your way back. Asking for help is the first step on your road out of debt.

My one big piece of advice here is to avoid like the plague any companies that offer you consolidation loans and more credit. What you need at this point is good advice, help and understanding, not more debt. Here are some useful organisations to talk to about your pathway out of debt:

Citizens Advice: This is a free advice service for everyone in the UK. There's loads of helpful information on their website about literally everything, but they are especially good at helping you out with advice on debt and financial problems. You can talk to real advisers online or go into your local branch. www.citizensadvice.org.uk

StepChange: This is a national debt charity that helps you get out of debt with free advice and guidance throughout the process. There's a useful Debt Remedy tool on their website and they offer tailored debt-remedy plans specifically for your individual needs. www.stepchange.org

Samaritans: If you are having suicidal thoughts or you fear that someone you know is thinking about suicide, call the Samaritans. They have specially trained experts who can talk you through this difficult time and give you support and guidance on dealing with your debts. www.samaritans.org

Mind: If you're worried about a spending addiction or any other kind of mental illness related to your financial situation or your relationship with money, Mind is the place to start. There's a lot of information on their website to help you determine whether or not you need help, as well as great advice for getting started with counselling or self-help. www.mind.org.uk

Key things to remember to keep your finances under control

To sum up, remember that all of the good practices I suggested in this chapter will help you keep your finances under control:

- Take the time to reflect on your money habits and where they come from.
- Learn to notice, and sit with, your feelings about money.
- Window-shopping can be fun in its own right, and spending money is optional.
- Pay off your debts before you try to save.
- Celebrate paying off debts.
- You don't have to deal with debt alone.

Part Five

The future's bright

You have probably noticed by now that I absolutely love saving money. I love deals, I love coupons, I love money off everything. But there is one thing I love even more than saving and that is saving up.

Have you ever noticed how when you are saving money because something is cheaper, it's just saving, but when you are saving for something special in life it's called 'saving up'? I think it is a great way to describe what you are doing – because when you are saving up, you are taking your life to new heights, lifting yourself, elevating your situation. Saving up takes you places, it makes you happy!

Saving up is about giving yourself goals, and giving your money a clear direction to go in. Remember the scarcity impulse I told you about on page 142? I explained how human beings are still programmed to think they need to grab everything they see in case they don't get another chance. Saving up is about moving past that impulse, rising above those unhelpful, subconscious habits that have us buying things we don't need, and prioritising our dreams and ambitions. Basically, saving up is about taking control of your destiny. And we all need a bit of that, don't we?

When you are saving up, you are taking your life to new heights, lifting yourself, elevating your situation. Saving up takes you places, it makes you happy!

The Art of Saving Up

Before you start

In just a sec I'm going to share everything I've learned about saving up and tell you how to get started on your saving journey. But first I want you to do a little checklist, because I'm hoping that by the time you are reading this, you will have tackled some or all of your debts. It just doesn't make sense to think about saving until you have paid off debts that are costing you money. As you can see from the diagram on page 163, it actually leaves you less well off if you are saving money at a lower rate of interest than you're being charged on your debt. Apart from a very few exceptional circumstances, which I will tell you about, it would be wrong of me to advise you to save money if you are still paying off debts.

So before we start, do this quick checklist to make sure you don't have any of these debts:

- ☐ Credit cards
- ☐ Store cards
- ☐ Outstanding balances on any 'pay later' services like Klarna and Clearpay
- ☐ Personal finance loans
- ☐ Overdrafts

All done? Congratulations! That is a massive win. Why? Well, not only do you no longer have to worry about keeping up with repayments and all the stress that comes with owing money, you can actually start to *save* money. And, for me, that is where the fun really starts!

The value of a slush fund

It's probably advice we've all heard before: have an emergency fund, a back-up pot of money. I call it my slush fund. I grew up knowing that you should put three months' living costs aside in a savings account, in case you lose your job or something big happens that you need money for. It could be major repairs on your house or an injury that keeps you off work, anything that is going to cost you a lot and comes out of nowhere! It makes total sense when you think about it, like having a spare tyre in the car in case you get a flat tyre.

Me being me, I've always preferred to have at least *six* months' worth of wages in the bank. It just makes me feel better, knowing it's there. Again, it's all about your attitude. What reassures you might be different from what someone else needs. The point is that you put some money aside in a good savings account and you don't touch it.

Top Tip: If you have a mortgage, it might be tempting to pay off a chunk of it if you've got the spares, instead of putting it in a slush fund. I am all for being mortgage-free, but remember that, once you pay into your mortgage, the money is gone. So if you have paid off your credit cards and loans, set up your slush fund next. Then if something happens, you've got the money put aside to pay your mortgage until you get back on your feet. It goes against what I said earlier about it costing you money to save if you've got debts, but this is an exception to the rule. In financial circles they call it a 'premium for liquidity', which basically means the cost of having that flexibility.

I know what you're going to say: easier said than done, right?! I hear you. It is really difficult to have the discipline to put money away when it's not for a clearly defined goal or anything remotely exciting like buying a house, and it's even more difficult not to touch it when you want (not need) something and you know it's just sitting there!

How to get your slush fund going

Here are my tips for getting your slush fund up and running and, most importantly, to avoid touching it:

- Make sure your debts (other than your mortgage and any interest-free credit) are paid off first – see the checklist on page 175. There's just no point in letting them build up while you are saving, even for a slush fund.

- Find a good, high-interest savings account, ideally one you can't access really easily. Ask your bank or building society about accounts that require a bit of notice to withdraw money (but not too much notice, otherwise you won't be able to get it if there really is an emergency). That way you can't spend it when you want to book a holiday or buy new carpets. Use my Want or Need Test (see page 137) if you are ever wavering on this.

- If you don't earn a salary, use my Hourly Rate Principle (see page 34) to work out your monthly wage and then multiply it times three (or six if you are like me!) to work out what you're aiming for.

- Remind yourself why you are doing this and what it is for. Write it down in your journal if you're keeping one, or put it on a sticky note on the fridge. This is about security and safety. Your slush fund is your financial wingman. Don't fly solo!

- Give the money you put into your slush fund a name. I call mine my Dead Money. Don't laugh! I just think giving it a name makes it more real, like a bill or something you have to pay, and therefore you take it seriously. Ever since I can remember, I've put Dead Money aside in the slush fund. It sounds a bit morbid, I know, but calling it dead helps me see it as untouchable. Give it a go! What will you call yours?

- Celebrate your achievement in putting money aside. Take yourself off for a nice bath, plant something in the garden or do whatever makes you happy (and doesn't involve spending wads of cash) to mark this occasion. It's a sign of personal growth and security; it means you are taking care of yourself and your family. That is worth celebrating!

Goals, goals, goals

Having a goal for your savings is so important. Ask anyone at the top of their game in business or sport and they'll tell you that setting goals is how you get results. Why? Because you can have all the good intentions, all the big ideas, all the wants and needs in the world, but unless you set yourself a goal that clearly defines what you want to achieve or where you want to be, you'll never really know if you've achieved it or not. It's a bit like leaving home in the morning with a vague idea that

Unless you set yourself a goal that clearly defines what you want to achieve or where you want to be, you'll never really know if you've achieved it or not.

you need to get to work. If you don't have a goal in mind (in this case a destination – your office), how are you ever going to get there?

In the branch of psychology called 'performance psychology' (which aims to optimise people's performance, especially when they are under pressure) there are generally three types of goal:

Process goals: These are goals about changing your behaviour. It could be that you want to commit to spending more time at the gym or doing something creative, or in the case of money it could be about developing a new habit like sticking to a saving budget. These kinds of goal are usually easy to control and depend on you, so you could call them 'easy wins'.

Performance goals: These goals relate to your personal 'performance'. You could decide you want to get your weight down to 10 stone or get a first-class degree or, if it's about money, you might want to save £1,000 for an amazing holiday. These goals are also almost entirely under your control, but they are typically harder to achieve.

Outcome goals: Based on the idea of achieving or winning something, these goals often tie in with your performance goals. They could involve getting a great job, having a baby or owning your dream home mortgage-free. Outcome goals are harder to reach because they often depend on outside factors such as the employment market, your partner's or your fertility or the property market. They're not impossible, they just require a bit extra to get there.

So how do you know what goals you should set? Well, no surprises for guessing what I'm going to say! Remember at the start of the book when we talked about looking after the pennies? It's the little things. Your outcome goals might be the big dream, the endgame, but you have to start with your process goals. Little steps. Nail your process goals, and you will find that your performance goals fall into place a lot easier. Nail your performance goals, and your outcome goals will happen. Let's look at how we can apply all of this to saving.

Setting your goals when saving up for a holiday

Holidays are a great example of how setting a goal can be so effective. If you don't have a goal in place, it's the kind of thing you will probably always put to the bottom of your list because you think you can't afford it. But having a goal or two can get you on that plane and off to far-away lands sooner than you think.

- Set your outcome goal. Let's say it's having £5k in the bank to pay for a trip to Mexico with the family.
- Identify your process goal. In this case it could be something as simple as making sure you put money aside once a week for your holiday. (Notice how you are already making progress simply by giving yourself that little task!)
- Decide what your performance goal is. This would be about how much money you put away each week. Will you save £5 a week because you think you won't notice it, or will you aim for £50 and really pull out all the stops to make it happen in the shortest possible time? The amount of money you can save is all about how hard you commit to the grind: your performance.

How much you save and how long it takes you to do it are, of course, entirely up to you. If you are like me, you will go full tilt on your performance goals and maximise every penny you can put away, but everyone is different. The main thing is that you get in the habit of setting yourself goals and achieving them.

DO THIS: Set yourself an outcome goal and write it down. It could be saving £5k for a dream holiday or £500 for a Gucci handbag – whatever floats your boat. Now write down a process goal and a performance goal that will help you get there.

Start with something small that will help you get into the groove of saving like this. If you're not someone who finds financial discipline easy, it will take some time to develop. It's like going to the gym or making your bed in the morning – good habits don't appear overnight. (Actually, making your bed in the morning does!)

Disciplinary action

Being motivated to do something is easy, but having the discipline to see it through is another thing entirely! Self-discipline is hard because it requires sacrifices – you have to do things even when you don't want to. When you're saving up for something, that means putting money away instead of buying that dress or eating out or doing what you want in the moment. Self-discipline is about going without in the short term because you know the long term is worth it. That's why you'll find that most successful people have a good dose of self-discipline. It takes time and commitment.

Top Tip: **Don't beat yourself up if you find it hard to save at first. Remember, it's like training at the gym or building a house: it doesn't happen overnight and it's not always fun. But it will come and it will be worth all your hard work in the end!**

Saving for the Big Things in Life

Now that you've mastered the art of saving, let's have a look at some of the big things in life that most of us will try to save for at some point.

Pensions

A pension is basically a savings account that you can't touch until you are 55 years old in the UK (it's going up to age 57 in 2028). When you're 55 you can access some of the cash in your pension, or you can get payouts from your pension like wages. There are loads of different pension plans – some are private, and some are done through your work where they pay into it at source (out of your wages).

And, of course, we all get a state pension here in the UK at the age of 66 (rising to 67 in 2026–2028). If you think you'd like to have a bit more in your pocket in your twilight years, then you will probably need to think about setting up an additional pension.

Top Tip: **You're not under any obligation to have a pension. You could invest your money in property or in stocks and shares if you prefer to have more independence about your money and how it's being made. Remember, a pension is really just a big savings account that you can't touch until you're older. I'd say a pension is a good idea for 99 per cent of people. It's a great way to ring-fence your savings and let them grow somewhere you can't access them. Especially if you're someone who lacks financial discipline and struggles to save. But it's not obligatory.**

The thought of putting money away and not being able to get at it for 30 years or so can seem quite daunting and/or unnecessary when you are young. It's so easy to think you've got years yet before you need to worry about pensions and retirement and all that boring stuff. But if being a mum has taught me anything it's that time waits for no one, and before you know it you're celebrating your 40th birthday! If you can find the discipline to think about your future, even if it feels like a million years away, you'll feel better about getting older, knowing that you've got the funds saved up for a comfortable retirement.

I'm not a qualified financial adviser, so I'm not going to give you specific pension advice here. Search online for your best local independent advisers or ask friends to recommend someone. I always think it's better to talk to someone in person if you can, rather than doing it online.

Pensions overview

Here are some key points about pensions that it will help you to know:

- A workplace pension is pretty much always a good idea in my opinion, as you never see the money – it goes straight out of your wages and into your pension fund. Even better, your employer will usually add some extra into the fund for you. Often you get tax relief from the government as well. I'm not saying you *must* do this, but it is usually a win-win situation. I've still got a pension from years ago when I worked in a bank, and even though I don't pay into it any more, I love getting the statements and seeing how the money has grown over the years.

Top Tip: **Remember, paying into a pension is like a mortgage in that, once you pay money into it, the money is gone (for a long while anyway). If you are trying to pay off debts, it might be worth putting your pension plans on hold until you've cleared the path a little bit.**

- If you are self-employed, you will need to get a private or personal pension. Get advice from an independent adviser about which one is right for you, as there are thousands of options.

- You can't 'pay in' to the state pension scheme in the way you can with private or workplace schemes, but you do need to make sure you are paying your National Insurance. It should all happen automatically, but check with your employer if you are in any doubt.

- Know who your pension is going to if you die.

- Make sure your pension is regulated by the Financial Conduct Authority or The Pensions Regulator. Again, a good independent adviser will be your friend here.

Saving for a deposit on a home

The numbers change over time but in general the average first-time buyer in the UK needs to find a deposit of around 20 per cent of the value of the home they are hoping to buy. So if you're looking at a flat for £100k, that means you've got to find £20,000 in hard cash before you can even think about getting a mortgage. That's difficult – even for someone like me, who loves saving!

It's not only about saving for the deposit. You need to know if you can actually afford to live in the home of your dreams. It's one thing getting a mortgage, but what's the point of living somewhere if you are constantly in debt and worrying about paying the bills?

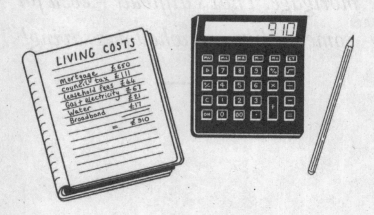

If you're looking at a flat for £100k, that means you've got to find £20,000 in hard cash before you can even think about getting a mortgage. That's difficult – even for someone like me, who loves saving!

Turbocharging the process

Most of the advice you read about saving for anything tells you to set a target figure and work out what you can afford each month to get to it. It might take you two years, it might take you five, but you will get there in the end. Well, that is true. But if you are like me and want to turbocharge your savings, you might prefer to do things a bit differently.

I like to work out exactly how much living in that house is going to cost me every month. I add up the mortgage, the council tax, the bills, any leasehold fees – everything that I'm going to have to spend each month on living there. Base this estimate of what your outgoings are likely to be on the kind of home you'd like to buy. You don't need to have exact figures – just use estimates where you don't know the correct amount. And that's the amount I like to save. Why? Because if I can't find that money now and put it away, how am I going to afford to live in the house I'm trying to buy? Getting myself used to that kind of sum going out every month helps me 'train' for the reality of owning a home – and it also helps me save a lot of money much faster.

I realise that isn't achievable for everyone, however. If you're paying rent on a place while trying to save, it's probably not going to be possible to find the cost of living in a whole extra home out of your pay packet.

When you're going for the big bucks like a deposit on a home, this is where all the other savings strategies I talked about in Part Three come into play. Take on the extra work, sell all of the clutter, rent out that garage if you've got one. Move back in with your parents if you can and if it means you'll save faster.

There are also now a lot of schemes that help first-time buyers get on the ladder, such as equity loans where the government basically chips in on your down payment. These are great, but remember you'll usually have to pay back the equity loan either a certain amount of time later or when you move on.

Meet LISA!

If you are aged 18–39 and saving for a deposit on a house, you can get a 25 per cent bonus from the government on your savings if you put your money in a Lifetime ISA (aka LISA.) This special ISA (see page 200 for more on ISAs) is great for first-time buyers. You can save up to £4,000 and the government will currently add a 25 per cent bonus on top. That's an extra £1,000 a year of free cash, before any interest! Ask your bank or building society about opening a LISA.

Making a baby fund

Babies are expensive! Don't get me wrong, it's absolutely the best thing I've ever done, having babies. But blimey they cost a lot! From the moment they are born (and actually well before, if you count all the extra food you eat and the maternity classes you go to), they cost a complete fortune!

Nappies, clothes, milk if you're not breastfeeding, dummies, toys, prams, cots…the list is endless. One of the things you can do to baby-proof your finances is set up a savings pot as soon as you know you are expecting. A bit like my mortgage-saving strategy, work out how much you think a baby is going to cost on a weekly or monthly basis and start squirrelling away that much as soon as you know the baby is on the way! This helps you get used to the kind of spending that is in store, and you will hopefully build up a nice nest egg for all your essentials.

Maybe you decide to put enough away every week for two packets of nappies and some wipes and nappy bags. That's currently going to be around £20.

£20 a week = £80 a month

£80 x 9 months = £720

£720 is going to come in very handy when your little bundle of joy arrives!

There are also other ways to make savings when your baby comes along:

Have a baby shower: My friends put on baby showers for me both times I was expecting. This is a great opportunity to ask your nearest and dearest for the things you will really need, so do not pass it up! People want to help and support you, so don't feel embarrassed about accepting gifts from your friends and family. It's all part of human nature, I think, to help young parents on their way. I was pretty extreme and asked for babygros in different sizes so that I had a couple of years' worth of them ready and waiting for the baby to grow into, and I didn't have to buy any for ages! But if you don't want to be explicit, you can always just exchange items you receive for other things that you think you might need.

DO THIS: Write a list of all the things you will need, not only when the baby comes along but a few months down the line. They don't have to be big expensive items. For me it was babygros, hats and socks — all the little things that they grow out of so quickly. Then when someone asks if there's anything you need, you'll have it front of mind to say, and you'll avoid getting gifts you don't necessarily need.

Buy second-hand everything: Babies grow so fast that it is just pointless buying new! NCT sales, eBay and other local organisations are usually pretty good places to find whatever you need, from prams and playmats to mobiles and sterilisers. The only things you absolutely have to buy new, for safety reasons, are car seats and mattresses.

Try breastfeeding if you can: I loved breastfeeding both of my babies – it's really good for their growth and immune system and all that stuff, but I especially loved it because it was free! I know it's not for everyone, but it's definitely worth a go and could save you hundreds of pounds over a year.

Use toy libraries and rental schemes: They are obviously much more economical than buying things you won't need for long. Better for your purse, better for the planet, and your children don't get bored with their toys!

Avoid expensive baby classes: These promise to make your baby cleverer or happier or whatever it is. They're a baby! They just want their mum and lots of cuddles and smiles. Go to your local church and community centre groups, NCT breastfeeding groups, whatever is on locally where you can meet other mums and have a cup of tea and a biscuit without spending £60 for them to be asleep all the way through it.

Make the most of freebies: New mums can get lots of freebies from the major nappy brands. The big baby forums like Emma's Diary and the NCT are good places to start.

Try cloth nappies

Have you considered using washable nappies? Washables have come a long way since we were little. These days they are slimline and really easy to use and wash (no soaking them in buckets like our mums did!). And, of course, they are better for the environment. Did you know that most of the disposable nappies we use are still made with non-biodegradable plastics and can sit in landfill for literally hundreds of years? Ew! It's also one of the reasons why disposable nappies are so expensive – we get charged a tax on them (around 10p per £1) for the recycling costs. Washables are not only a great alternative for the planet but can also save you money over time. While there's an initial outlay for the nappies and the kit, most estimates reckon you can save around £2,000 over the time your child is in nappies. That is not to be sniffed at! And, of course, if you have another baby you have already got all the kit. A lot of local councils also encourage new parents to use washables by offering cash incentives and free local laundry-collection services. Check what your local council is doing and see if washables can work for you.

A word about ISAs

Much of the jargon around money seems to be deliberately confusing, doesn't it? ISA stands for Individual Savings Account, so you might think it's the same as a savings account, right? But ISAs are actually slightly different to regular savings accounts in that they offer you tax-free savings. This means that with an ISA you can save up to a maximum amount each year (£20,000 in 2021) without having to pay tax on the interest you earn on it. If you had that same amount of money in a regular savings account, you might have to pay tax on the interest you earned on it. I know, confusing!

To make things even more complicated, there are different types of ISA. The two main types are the cash ISA (which is just putting your money into an account and letting it sit there and earn interest) and the stocks and shares ISA (which is where your money gets invested on the stock market, which means you take on a bit more risk but the overall gains are usually higher). For cash ISAs, you have to be 16 years or over, and for stocks and shares ISAs 18 or over. There are also other kinds like innovative finance ISAs (for age 18 or over), lifetime ISAs (for 18 or over but under 40) and junior ISAs (for under 18). ISAs known as fixed rate ISAs and notice ISAs are types of cash ISA.

Whether or not an ISA is any better than a simple savings account will depend on the amount of money you want to put in there, how quickly you want to be able to access it and even what you are saving for. Every bank and building society has many different ISA products, so take your time, do your research and work out what's best for you.

Top Tip: You can transfer ISAs in the same way as for credit cards and loans, so keep an eye out for transfer deals and you could save quite a bit. Remember, the money always needs to be transferred by the bank or building society – you can't simply take it out of one and put it into another yourself, as that would basically be opening a new account and so would be treated as part of the annual new ISA limit, meaning that different rules apply.

Try this fun way to save every day

Here's a little thing I do every day just because I like saving. I shared it on my Instagram a while ago and loads of my followers liked it, too. I think it's because it's just moving little amounts into savings, so it seems really easy and achievable, and gets big results quite quickly. This is not a savings method that has been devised by economists or financial advisers, it's just a little trick of the mind really, that gets you into good habits and you can do in two secs from your phone.

Look at your bank balance every day, and whatever the last figure is, transfer it over to your savings account. So if there's £208 in your current account, transfer £8 into your savings account. If the next day there's £54 in the current account, put £4 into your savings. It's amazing how quickly you'll find yourself saving £30 or £40 a week without missing it and over time that really adds up.

	M	Tu	W	Th	F	Sa	Su
MY BANK ↓ IN TO SAVING	£104 ↓ £4	£211 ↓ £1	£56 ↓ £6	£85 ↓ £5	£42 ↓ £2	£73 ↓ £3	£308 ↓ £8

= £29

£29 × 52 weeks = £1508 saved!

Key things to remember when saving for the big things in life

To sum up, follow this advice for safe saving:

- Be debt-free before you start saving (unless your debts are interest-free).

- Set up a slush fund and call it something (mine is Dead Money).

- Give yourself savings goals – money needs direction or else it will get lost.

- If saving for a home, get in training by putting aside the amount you will realistically need to live on.

- Be prepared! Pensions, baby funds and anything else that gives you time to save for something in the future are always a good idea.

Part Six

Difficult conversations and getting the family involved

I am so proud of everything I have achieved, as Money Mum on Instagram and now this book. Writing it is one of the best things I've ever done and I am so happy you are reading it!

But what I am proudest of is being a mum to my two amazing kids. I know all mums feel this way about their children, it's not just me. They're just the best and I love them so much it's unbelievable.

My family is my world. That's why on my social media you'll see me posting as much about my family life and the kids as you will money-saving tips and advice. I can't really do one without the other. They are two sides of the same coin: building financial security for my family is all part of being the best mum I can be.

Every parent wants the best for their children. What does the best mean? To me the best doesn't mean handing everything to them on a plate, but giving them the awareness, the tools and the mindset to find their own version of success in life. It also means providing security – not in the sense that they think they'll never have to earn their own money, but in the sense that you have got their back, and are here to guide them and show them the way.

Building financial security for my family is all part of being the best mum I can be.

Building Financial Security

And of course there's Money Dad, Adam, at my side. I'm not sure I could have done any of it without him. He has been so supportive and such a rock; it's not just a public persona, he really is a wonderful dad and my partner in everything – especially saving money! We are very much in sync when it comes to our finances, and I think that is so important when you are deciding whether to settle down with someone or not.

Play to your individual strengths

One of the things that really work with me and Adam is that we have always played to our strengths. What do I mean by that? Well, I see so many relationships even today where the man feels he has to be the big provider and the woman thinks she's got to be a domestic goddess from the 1950s and have dinner on the table every night. I'm not saying either of those things is bad, but if it's not playing to your strengths, as a couple you're missing a trick.

Today, all the old gender rules have gone out the window! If you're a woman with an amazing business that takes up all your time and your other half is really good at cooking and getting everyone organised, then embrace that and don't worry about what you are 'supposed' to be! Nothing is for ever, so maybe in a few years' time you'll swap, or your partner's skills will come in handy in different ways later on. Many people are so limited by gender stereotypes – forget that and ask yourselves instead what your strengths are as individuals in a partnership. You might be surprised by what you discover!

DO THIS: Write a list of the skills you each have and the things you enjoy doing or think you'd like to do in the future. Treat it like you would a meeting or a career appraisal at work. Find out what is making you happy or miserable, what you'd like to do more or less of and how you see the future, and then decide together where you're going to go from here. Maybe you'll realise that one of you needs to retrain, or the other one is struggling with the burden of being the main breadwinner. It might be something as simple as one of you wanting to start saving more, or you might decide it's time to move home. Write down a few action points and agree to discuss things again after a certain time. People use these strategies all the time in the workplace and the corporate world, yet so often at home we just carry on blindly without stopping to think about what we are good at and where we are going. You don't even need to be in a couple to do this! If you're single or living with friends, or whatever your situation is, take some time to review and consider whether you are making the most of your talents.

Things weren't always plain sailing for me and Adam, and in many ways the story of how we got together is also the story of how I have come to build financial security. We met on a dating site and after we'd had a few dates, I was smitten. I knew he was the one and I wanted to do everything I could to make sure he and I stayed the distance. But then Adam dumped me – by text! I couldn't believe it, I was so certain he was the one. In my head I'd already got the wedding all planned and had picked out a colour scheme for the bridesmaids, bought the house, the works. And then he dumped me! I'll never forget what he said: that he was 95 per cent certain that it wasn't going to work out between us.

Me being me, I looked at that number on my phone screen – 95 per cent – and I thought, well, there's still a 5 per cent chance then! And I worked at it, chipped away to bring that number down. I won't go into details here but let's just say I didn't give up, I kept my eyes on the prize, and eventually Adam realised he'd made a bit of an error! We got back together and got married in 2014.

More than a decade after we met, we are as strong as ever. We are getting older, though, and we've had some difficult conversations as a couple and as parents. What happens if one of us dies? What if one of us gets ill? Or we both die? What happens if everything we have worked for disappears?

Facing Up to the Future

No one wants to have these conversations, do they? I think it's part of human nature to avoid the subject of death. People don't like to think about losing the people they care about, or going before their time. No one likes leaving the party early (unless you are me and you actually do like leaving the party early – I like being in bed by 9pm!).

These difficult topics don't apply only to people who are married or have children. Everyone, no matter what their circumstances, has a future to plan for, people to think about and look after. We are all connected to others somehow, whether it's an ageing parent, a really good friend or even a loved pet or favourite charity. And I really believe that we all need to have the tough conversations about what happens in the event of the unthinkable.

Like pensions and insurance and all the other so-called boring aspects of getting your finances together, it is easy to put these decisions to the bottom of the to-do list. But it is so

For me, planning for the future and protecting the things and people who are important is all part of being able to find peace and joy in the present.

important to address these things. It seems like now more than ever we are bombarded with messages about living for the moment and being present with ourselves and our families, rather than worrying about a future we can't control.

For me, planning for the future and protecting the things and people who are important is all part of being able to find peace and joy in the present. I see it as a bit like going on holiday: choosing where you'll go, thinking about what you'll take with you, saving up money so you can have a nice time while you are there, taking safety precautions when you travel, making sure the house is locked and someone waters the plants while you are away. These are all processes we take for granted when we are planning a break. So why don't we give the same thought and attention to planning how we will keep things safe when we are not there?

I can't tell you how to approach these issues – everyone's life and circumstances are different. But here are my thoughts on some of the big issues around family and finances, which you may find useful.

Is a joint account a good idea?

A lot of my followers ask me whether I think it's a good idea to get a joint account with their partner or spouse. Everyone's situation is different so I can't tell you what to do. But I will

say that I have always had my own bank account, and as a woman and a breadwinner in the 21st century, I really value having my financial independence. Having separate accounts doesn't mean you're not committed or can't take a shared approach to your finances as a couple.

Plusses

If you're thinking about whether to get a joint account, some of the upsides are as follows:

- Financial transparency with your partner.
- Awareness of being in it together, which can help avoid arguments about money.
- Convenience of having bills, mortgage and other household stuff in one space.

Minuses

It's obviously also important to consider some of the downsides:

- Joint responsibility for debts, overdrafts, loans.
- Because of 'co-scoring', your credit history affected by theirs and vice-versa.
- No protection for your money if your partner empties the account.

On balance, I'm not saying you need to worry about whether your new husband is likely to run off with all the money from your joint account – that's not very romantic, I know! All I'm saying is, think carefully about whether you really *need* to set up a joint account and expose each other unnecessarily to problems like your credit score.

If you intend to share the household finances and running costs, it is just as easy to agree how you are going to split the bills and to each take responsibility for doing so. You might agree to split everything 50/50. Or it could be that one of you pays for the energy and the other one buys the shopping. If one of you is earning a lot more than the other, then maybe it's about agreeing a 70/30 split or similar. However you come to an agreement, the important thing is that you come to one and you both keep your side of the bargain. That's what being in a partnership is about, after all.

Saying I do

I love being Mrs Bird but I know marriage isn't for everyone. Rightly or wrongly, the government does try to encourage couples to get married by offering them tax breaks and other incentives to tie the knot. While I would never suggest you get married for the tax breaks, if you are wondering whether to marry or enter into a civil partnership with your loved one, and you're curious to know about the financial aspect, here are a few key points:

- You can get a bigger state pension when your spouse dies, and many workplace pensions pass on benefits to the surviving spouse that they might not do to an unmarried partner. Check with your pension provider about what happens if one of you dies.

- If you're married and your spouse dies, you don't have to pay inheritance tax on anything you receive.

- You can get tax breaks if one of you is a non-taxpayer or earns below their Personal Allowance, and the other one pays the basic rate. Find out more on the HMRC website: https://www.gov.uk/marriage-allowance

Making a will

I know, I know, this is the worst possible job on your to-do list – and so easy to put off for another day. But you have got to do this! I see it as a bit like making your bed in the morning or leaving your desk tidy at the end of day. It might be easier to just get up and leave it in a mess, but you will feel a lot better, and like you have achieved a small victory, if you spend five minutes making it shipshape.

The other thing I would say is to let everyone know what your wishes are. If you really want to leave it all to the cats' home, then make sure your family knows that this is your intention (although it goes without saying that I really hope you won't leave it *all t*o the cats' home, as much as I like cats). It will save everyone a lot of heartache and expensive solicitors' fees if people know what's coming.

Actually making a will is fairly straightforward and your local solicitor can guide you through it. How much it costs you will depend on how complex your will is, who you are leaving what to and how. There are also plenty of online will-writing services but I would recommend talking to a solicitor, especially if you have children and a home and/or any other assets.

You should also check out Free Wills Month. It takes place every year in October and is a great way to get your will done for free by a qualified solicitor. You access the service via one of the charities taking part (all the big national charities get involved and lots of smaller local ones, too). The idea is that in return for having your will done for free, you leave a legacy (some money) to the charity. It doesn't have to be much, and it's not obligatory. But if there is a charity you feel strongly about and you have the ability to leave them something in your will, it's a good way to get this difficult job done while also feeling like you're doing a good thing.

https://freewillsmonth.org.uk

Getting your house in order

It can also be really handy to keep a record of where all your accounts are, so that your executors (the people sorting everything out when you are gone) can find all the details they'll need. If you have set up a spreadsheet like the one me and Adam have, you could share that with the person you think will be handling everything. That way they can tie up all the loose ends and make sure your money isn't still paying bills to the gas company when you're not around anymore. If you haven't got a spreadsheet, even just a piece of paper with a list of all your accounts will be helpful for the executors. Horrible to think about, I know, but it's about looking after your loved ones and making a difficult time that little bit easier.

If you find you are regularly putting this task off, especially if you are single or don't have children to pass your money on to, try making it a bit fun to do. Maybe you and a mate who needs to do the same thing can get together and put some music on and go through it all together. If you are a couple, have a great meal at home, put some candles on the table, have a glass of wine and make it a date night. It could be as simple as giving yourself a treat of some sort once you have done it all. Whatever it takes, just try to prioritise getting yourself sorted out on this front. Trust me, there is a real sense of calm to be had once you have all your affairs in order, so enjoy that feeling.

Life insurance – what's that?

Life insurance is a way of covering all your costs should you die. There are loads of different options and types of cover, but generally speaking it pays off your mortgage and any other debts you might have, and gives your children or other dependants some money for when you're not around. If you haven't got children, I'd say it's not really worth it. But if you have, and you have a mortgage, it can be a great way to ensure all that worry is taken care of.

Top Tip: Get started early. Life insurance gets more expensive as you get older. (Why? Because you are more likely to die the older you get, so the risk to the insurer is higher and they charge you more for taking that risk.) If you are in your forties or fifties and have paid off a large part of your mortgage or are mortgage-free like me, it can be worth weighing up whether life insurance is worth the monthly cost or whether other options, like putting money into an ISA, would be better for your finances (as you'd still have access to the money if you needed it). Paying into an insurance policy is like paying off a mortgage, in that once you make that payment it is gone. If you are struggling to make ends meet every month, there might be another way to do it.

As always, it is important to discuss this with an independent financial adviser, who will assess your situation and give you the best advice for your particular circumstances.

Involving the Children

Hopefully all the difficult stuff we have just been talking about is a long way off for us! Something much nicer and happier, but just as important, to think about is getting the children and other young people in your life on board with saving.

What's the point in being a good saver if you're not passing on some of your new skills to the next generation, eh? As you know, I was brought up to respect money and I never took

I'm not here to tell you what they should and shouldn't have, but you can still teach your children the value of money and help them understand exactly how to make theirs last.

a penny for granted. But even back then I was the odd one out. Nowadays children expect so much: gaming consoles, holidays, nice clothes, phones, tablets. I'm not here to tell you what they should and shouldn't have, but you can still teach your children the value of money and help them understand exactly how to make theirs last.

Motivating kids

The first thing to say is that this need not be boring. Saving can be fun for children if you make it a bit exciting and something they can look forward to. If they get money for their birthday and you just put it in the bank without telling them, your children are not going to get that excited about the idea of saving, are they? But if you let them go into the bank, give the money to the cashier and look at their balance afterwards and you make a bit of a fuss about it, suddenly it's something grown-up and important for them to do.

Both of my children have piggy banks that they were given as christening presents, and whenever the piggy banks get full we take them down to the bank and the kids pay it all in to their savings accounts. They both really love doing it, and I love watching them enjoy the saving process. Queuing up at the bank and pouring all their coins into the drawer, seeing the cashier count all the cash really fast, checking their balance afterwards – it's an exciting event for them, and something we all look forward to doing.

Top Tip: **You don't need to be a parent to do this! It's a fun thing to do with little ones if you are a grandparent, godparent, cousin, aunty, uncle or good friend. I know how busy being a mum or dad can be and sometimes we just don't have the time to spend a morning paying a load of copper coins into the bank. Why not start a little saving club with your relatives or godchildren and notice how much joy you get from teaching them good habits? Their parents will thank you for it as well.**

A lot of people ask me the best age to start saving with their children. I don't know if there is a perfect age, to be honest. Every child is different, but most of them do start showing an interest in money at some point. Why wouldn't they? They see us using it in almost every part of daily life, from paying for school dinners and buying ice cream in the park to collecting money at the school fête and paying to go into theme parks. They learn early on that money is part of most situations they're involved in. You'll know when the time is right to start talking money with your children. The important thing is that you make good associations with saving and get them to start paying attention to money.

Why so important? Not necessarily because you want them to have lots of it! No one ever thought a five-year-old on the loose with a big wad of cash was a good idea. It's more because saving is such an important skill to have. It teaches children how to wait for something, it teaches them self-discipline and foresight, and it gives them a sense of achievement when they reach their savings goals. And that all contributes to self-esteem, which is what we want for our kids, right?

Going to the bank with the contents of a piggy bank is one way to start saving. But how do we motivate our children to save, now that so much of our financial life takes place by card and on our phones? It's a tricky one, but I think you can still talk about money to young children, especially when you are doing

transactions that involve spending, where they understand that you are receiving something in return for your money. When you spend some money with your children, take a second to look at the transaction on your app if you are using your phone, or at your receipt if you have paid by card, and talk through what you have just spent and what you have spent it on. It might be that the numbers are beyond their understanding at this point, but that doesn't really matter. It's more about getting them used to the idea that every transaction has a consequence. You don't get cinema tickets by magic (although you almost do, if you sign up for a certain meerkat-based app!).

Opening a child's bank account

Don't worry if you haven't started saving with your kids! I know loads of people who get cheques and money at Christmas from the grannies and grandads and they still haven't put them in the bank by Easter. I know people who don't have savings accounts for their children at all. But I do think it's a good idea to open an account for children if you can, if only because the interest rates for them are typically higher than the rubbish ones we adults get.

Opening a bank account for a child has these key advantages:

- The money is protected so it can't be eaten away. (I know someone whose son got £100 cash for Christmas and they never got around to paying it in to the bank – they left it in his piggy bank in his room. One day they realised he'd spent it all, buying sweets and chocolate on the way home from school!)

- Children can watch their savings grow on an app or in their statements and begin to feel what it's like to have a bit of money behind them.

- They can begin to understand interest rates, too. Get them to keep an eye on theirs and see if they can work out how it affects their balance.

Top Tip: The features of children's accounts vary with the bank or building society, and some children's accounts can be opened at a younger age than others. Do the research and get yourself the best deal – don't just open an account with your own bank because that's the one you know. It might be great for you but not as great when it comes to children's accounts.

Junior ISA or savings account?

Children's savings accounts and junior ISAs both work in pretty much the same way these days – check with your bank or building society or go online to find the best rates and options for your child. The only big difference is that with a Junior ISA the money is locked away until they are 18 and then it is theirs – you don't have any control over what happens to it once they are 18. The hope is that they'll use it for something good like tuition fees or starting a business, but you don't get to stop them if they want to spend it all on designer clothes and Nando's for all their friends. You therefore need to consider whether that is something you are OK with. The plus side is that they can't withdraw it until they are 18, so there is less temptation to dip into it over the years.

There are also restrictions in place on children's savings accounts, to stop parents from using their kids' accounts to avoid taxes. It's complicated, and the rules change over time, so talk to your financial adviser or at least make sure you do all the research before you open your child's saving account.

Making allowances

Don't worry if you haven't done any of this with your kids yet. I firmly believe it is never too late to get them interested in saving money. In fact, as they get older, they will start to want certain things more – the phones and the accessories and all of that – which can be great motivators for starting to save.

As I said at the beginning of this book, getting an allowance when I was a teenager (and knowing there wasn't any more secret money on a magic tree for me when it ran out) had a really big impact on me. It shaped the way I look at money and made me appreciate the value of every single penny.

My children are still too young for pocket money or an allowance. But I know that when the time comes I'll start giving them small amounts of cash on a regular basis, first as weekly pocket money and later as a monthly allowance.

I know some people think that giving children pocket money or an allowance is wrong because it's giving them 'free' money that they haven't earned. A lot of parents I meet give their kids chores and jobs to earn their pocket money. I read about one family who charged their five-year-old daughter rent and bills and deducted it from her weekly $5 pocket money. I'm all for getting them started early!

Actually I'm a big advocate for pocket money and allowances, even, or maybe I mean especially, without the chores, and here's why:

- An allowance gives a child responsibility. From physically looking after cash in their purse or wallet to making 'mature' decisions about what is necessary and what they can live without, it makes them think about and take care of their money.

- Allowances and pocket money teach children that money is not infinitely available to them, even if they are doing chores to earn it (much like wages).

- They can still do chores and jobs to earn extra money if there is something they really want.

- Earning money only in exchange for chores can be demotivating for children, whose interest you risk losing if a bit of pocket money is only ever available to them when they unload the dishwasher.

- Paying children money for being helpful around the house can also backfire on you, and you may end up with a kid who will only do something if you offer to pay them for it. Not ideal!

Prepaid pocket-money cards: what do we think of them?

We are all using debit cards and other digital ways to transfer money more nowadays. With services like Apple Pay and Google Pay on our phones, and new gadgets enabling practically anyone to take a card payment, it has never been easier to live a cash-free life. The Covid-19 pandemic accelerated the move to cashless, with shops keen to avoid physical contact with customers as much as possible.

A number of prepaid, debit-style pocket-money cards and apps for children have sprung up over the past few years. These cards are preloaded with money (like a credit card, only as the parent you are the provider of the credit, or in this case the pocket money) and your child can use the card to pay for things in shops and online, just like they would with cash.

The big sell for parents and families is that you can see exactly where they are spending their money (you also have the app) and you can easily top up their funds from your own online bank account. You can also set them chores and saving goals, and other family members can pay in to their pocket-money accounts. It's kind of halfway to a bank account, without actually being one.

I can totally see why they are handy. They can, in theory at least, help children learn to develop certain good behaviours around money, like checking their balance and seeing how it is impacted when they buy a packet of sweets. They can also start to use ATMs.

But I can't help feeling that giving children these cards as their first experience of pocket money is missing out a vital element of it: holding physical cash in their hands and learning to look after it. This is not something we talk about a lot, but I think children need to learn how money feels in their hands and pockets. To hear the clinking sound of coins in their piggy banks and in the shopkeeper's tills. Why? Because all the senses can make really powerful associations and can impact our memory for years to come. I still remember the sound of the pennies jingling around in my old coffee jar when I was a girl. Without that sense of money being something physical and real, which can be touched and heard and even smelled, we're not giving children a chance to make those long-lasting associations with money and to see it as an actual thing, rather than just a concept. And we all know it's easier to look after something if you can see and feel it.

Of course, you can combine the two. Using a pocket-money card doesn't mean they can't also have cash. I just think that for their very first pocket money, nothing beats the real thing. There's plenty of time for cards and online banking when they are older.

How much pocket money?

Not sure how much pocket money you should be giving your children? It will depend on all sorts of things, like where you live, how old they are and what their mates are getting. But my advice is to go for just a little bit less than you think they would be happy with. If you think they would like £3 a week, give them £2. That way, they'll have to be a bit more careful about the way they spend it, and they can try to earn the extra by using their initiative.

I am by no means saying that it's good to grow up poor, but did you know that some of the world's wealthiest people have come from extremely humble beginnings? From Oprah Winfrey and Roman Abramovich to Amancio Ortega (the founder of Zara) and Jan Koum (co-founder of WhatsApp), at least two thirds of the world's billionaires faced difficult circumstances in childhood but went on to do amazing things and earn unbelievable amounts of money. There is something very powerful in the hardship of a tough beginning that drives some – not all – people to succeed in later life. Remember that next time your children are nagging you for that extra pound!

However much you decide to give them, and whether you go for a pocket-money card or old-fashioned cash, here are my three golden rules for giving children pocket money or an allowance:

- Agree an amount you will give them and stick to it.
- Agree a time when you will review the amount and stick to it.
- Stick to it.

(PS: Make sure you stick to it!)

Family matters

Remember these key points with regard to family finances:

- Play to your strengths in relationships and ditch the old-fashioned ideas about gender roles and money.
- Give careful consideration to opening a joint account.
- No one likes to think about death but it happens.
- Being prepared helps – make a will.
- Pocket money and allowances for children are important.
- Giving them extra if they ask could be making a rod for your own back, and theirs.

Part Seven

Money isn't everything
(and I really mean that)

The world stopped for everyone in the spring of 2020, didn't it? Like people all around the world, me and my family went into lockdown, an experience I had never, ever imagined would happen in my lifetime.

I can remember watching the news and just being speechless. It all seemed so unreal. It still does in a way – it's kind of hard to believe it really happened.

I know I'm not alone when I say I struggled with so many aspects of life during that time: I felt overwhelmed and hopeless one day, angry and frustrated the next. I think it was the uncertainty of not knowing when it would end and of trying to keep everyone safe. I couldn't deal with home schooling at all! Bronte was still a baby, and as anyone who has had a baby knows, they are all-consuming. I don't know how they do it as they can't even walk, but they just need you all the time! Feeding, changing, playing, cleaning up, and you are constantly tired because of lack of sleep. Trying to home school Brody at the same time, being there for him, trying to put on a brave face and protect him from the worries we were all having, wasn't easy at all. Because I struggle with anxiety and low mood, on some days I just wanted to stay in bed and hide under the duvet until it had all gone away.

But it was also a time to reflect on the way we lived. Our

_____

Lockdown taught me some really valuable lessons, and gave me time and space to reflect on what I was trying to achieve as Money Mum.

_____

world got smaller – it was just the four of us at home, with no days out, no holidays, nothing to get dressed up for, no one to entertain and nothing much to spend money on except food and comfy clothes. I remember being really surprised by the little things that I missed, like wearing my summer wedges! I didn't have a reason to wear them all summer. Sometimes I put them on in the garden, just because I wanted to feel like I was going out somewhere.

Looking back, I also realise how much I learned going through that whole experience. I would never wish for any of us to have to be in lockdown again, but I know it taught me some really valuable lessons, and gave me time and space to reflect on what I was trying to achieve as Money Mum. What would 'success' look like for me? What is it all for in the end?

Financial Security

We have always enjoyed going on walks – people don't realise how much absolutely beautiful countryside there is in Essex – and as a family we like to get out and be in nature whenever we can. It's such a simple (and, let's not forget, free) way to spend time together. So many of my own happiest childhood memories are of going to the woods or the park, running around without a care. Don't get me wrong, I love going to children's soft play and having a coffee (which I have brought with me, of course) with my friends while the kids play, but there's nothing quite like the fresh air and the freedom of being outside with your kids. They love it and nothing makes parents happier than seeing their kids happy.

I also know that when I'm feeling low, going out for a walk and getting my body moving and breathing in the fresh air really helps me shift and process those negative thoughts and feelings. I can honestly say I have never come back from a walk feeling worse than when I went out!

In lockdown I noticed how our daily walks took on a new kind of meaning. They became these pockets of freedom and space, a time when we could enjoy the little things together: the birds in the trees, the clouds in the sky, the fresh air… I know it all sounds like a bit of a cliché, but clichés are clichés because they are true, aren't they? We stopped and we breathed, we let all the madness go and we really appreciated the little things, and each other. I loved all of that.

It was also a time when I had been working really hard at being Money Mum. My page had only been going for a year or so, and my 17k Instagram follower count was already a number I could never have imagined. I actually managed

to keep growing my account throughout lockdown, possibly because I had a message that people needed and wanted to hear at that time. We were all facing such a lot of uncertainty, with people losing their jobs, being furloughed, taking mortgage holidays, not knowing how to pay their bills. All my money-saving tips and bits of advice here and there were really ways to make everyone feel a bit more in control and less worried about it all.

I learned many things through those first months of lockdown, but the main thing was that it made me realise that money *can* buy you happiness. I know, I know – we're not supposed to say that! And, of course, you can't buy the special people in your life, you can't pay your way into friendship or romance. The smile on my children's faces, the way it feels to hold their hands, the deep bond I share with Adam – that's all priceless. None of what I've achieved as Money Mum would mean a thing to me without the people I love in my life.

But I do believe that having enough money to pay for your life, whether that is £1,000 a month or £10,000, and to live without the worry and fear and dread of being in debt, that *is* a kind of happiness that can be bought. It's not jumping-around-for-joy happiness, or crying-tears-of-laughter happiness, but it is peace of mind. It's a quiet happiness, a sense of calm and of being in control. And there is no shame in wanting that. One of my biggest hopes is that we can all start talking more openly about money, and how it is linked to our sense of security and, yes, happiness.

I know that my mum and dad won't mind me saying here that it used to make them both physically sick with worry, not knowing if they would be able to pay the bills every week when me and my sister Natalie were small. They just wanted to be able to provide the basics: the house, the water and the electricity, the food on the table. The things that make human beings feel safe. If you are worrying that you can't provide those things, whether for yourself or your family, then that is going to make you anxious and stressed.

Knowing that Adam and I had a float, the slush fund, to get us through lockdown was a genuine comfort to me. It was one less thing to worry about, at a time when there really were some very big things to worry about! Adam always says the only constant in life is change, and he is so right. If the pandemic taught us anything, it was that you just never know what is coming. Nothing stays the same. It's impossible to completely protect yourself from something you can't even imagine, but having that back-up of knowing you can put food on the table whatever happens is at least a small comfort.

Taking its toll

Stress really can make you physically ill. Even though we have evolved into 21st-century humans, with the internet and Uber, our bodies still process stress in the same way our ancestors did when they were living wild, running away from scary animals who might eat them. Our heart rate goes up, our immune system gets strained trying to protect us, and we lose concentration while we focus on the danger in front of us, in this case debts or lack of money.

Mutual Support

I've also realised just how important it is to support and lift up the other women out there who are trying to build businesses and brands, be amazing mothers and raise good children – oh, and change the world at the same time. I love being a mum and I love what I do, I love my home and family, and I love being out there in the world being me! I love it all and I want it all! But I'm not going to lie, it's really hard to keep the balancing act going at times. I know so many women who feel the same way, stretched in all directions! Us girls need to recognise the struggle we all face every day, and show each other compassion and support, not try to put each other down. We are all just humans trying our best to get on in the world. If you can help someone by making a nice comment, liking a post, sharing a profile – why wouldn't you do that? As I said earlier, lifting someone else up won't bring you down.

As I'm writing this, we are hoping that the worst of the pandemic is behind us. We are all coming out of our homes

—

*We are all just humans trying our
best to get on in the world.*

—

and meeting up with our friends and loved ones again. I am so pleased to see freedom and I can't wait to get out there again. I'm especially excited about going on holiday! But like all of us, I'm going back into the world with fresh eyes and a new sense of what it feels like to be isolated and alone.

I'm hoping that we'll all reach out a little bit more when we think someone is struggling, whether it's with money or mental health, or both. As someone who has worked in jobs at almost every level of prestige and pay, from mushroom picker to estate agent and now as Money Mum, I know how lonely it can be to feel like you don't have any status in this world, or like you'll never make enough money to get to where you want to be, or that everyone else thinks they're better than you. I'm also here to tell you that none of us is better than anyone else; at the end of the day, we're all just out there trying to pay our bills and provide for our loved ones. I find it so upsetting when I see people looking down on other people because of their job or their car or whatever. None of us is more special or important than anyone else in my opinion.

Encouragement, support, empathy and compassion around money and around mental health – these are all themes that are important to me and that I hope to develop further as I continue on my journey as Money Mum. (Oh, and don't forget having a laugh!) There's so much I want to

Encouragement, support, empathy and compassion around money and around mental health – these are all themes that are important to me.

do, and still so much more to learn and share with you all. But you'll have to watch this space for now!

Until then, I hope this book has helped you feel that even those of us who think we have absolutely no money to spare can start to save by making the tiniest of changes. Even when you think there's no point in trying, there's loads of help and advice out there to help you get back on track — you are definitely not alone.

That's all for now, but head over to Instagram for more money-saving advice, or even if you just fancy a chat.

Happy saving!

Gemma
x.
Money Mum

Gemma's

Glossy Glossary

I always make it clear to my Instagram followers that I am not a qualified financial adviser in the vein of someone like MoneySavingExpert Martin Lewis (who, I have to say, I think is brilliant and I love) or any of the other financial experts you might see on TV or in the papers. I'm just a mum from Essex who happens to be really good at saving.

However, because I spend such a lot of my time researching deals and markets and money-saving opportunities, it's fair to say I'm well acquainted with a lot of the jargon you get around money and saving. I have also worked as an estate agent and in a bank and, of course, I'm a mum, so when it comes to the lingo I've always made it my business to know what things mean in real terms (not in what I call 'money language'). In addition, because I'm dyslexic, seeing things written down isn't always the best way for me to understand them – I've learned to understand money and all its associated processes in a way that makes it easy and simple to digest, often without anything in front of me to look at.

With all of that in mind, I thought it would be useful to share with you my definitions for some of the key terms and phrases you come across in money-land. I've put this list together based on the questions I get asked by my followers (the financial ones anyway!). If there's anything I haven't covered, head over to Instagram and ask me!

What's APR, Gem?

It stands for Annual Percentage Rate and it's the cost of borrowing money. When you take out a credit card or a loan or a mortgage or anything like that, you will be charged by the company who is lending you the money. It will usually be a percentage of the amount you are borrowing. So if you are borrowing £100 and the APR for that loan is 25 per cent, you're being charged £25 for the loan, and when you pay it back you'll be paying £125 in total. Generally speaking, the lower your APR, the better.

APR is not the same as interest rate, but it includes your interest rate plus any other costs like set-up costs and compound interest. (Hold on, we'll get to that one in a minute!)

What are arrears, Gem?

This is a posh way of saying that a payment is overdue. If you're meant to pay your mortgage every month and you missed last month's payment, your account is in arrears. As a rule we don't want to be in arrears, OK?

Balance transfer card

This is a credit card that offers you a 0 per cent interest rate when you move your existing balance from another credit card. It is a great way to stop paying interest on existing card debts and can really help you get the balance down on your debts. However, the 0 per cent interest rate is usually only for a limited period of time, so you need to be aware of when it ends and either pay off your debt before then, or move it to another 0 per cent credit card before you start paying interest.

Bank account or building society?

They both do the same jobs: look after your money and lend you money. But a bank is a privately or publicly owned company, usually with branches all over the country, whereas a building society is owned by its members (like a co-operative society) and often doesn't have national branches (although a couple of well-known ones do). Usually people think of banks as somewhere you keep your day-to-day money and the building society as the place where you save. But they all offer so many different ways of saving these days, it is worth forgetting preconceptions and considering which place will give you the best deal, regardless of whether it is a bank or a building society.

What does it mean when you go bankrupt, Gem?

When you have a lot of debt that you can't pay back, going bankrupt is an option that can help you write off your debts. But it's not without its consequences – you may still have to make monthly payments and you'll probably struggle to get credit for a long time. I hear a lot of people talk quite flippantly about bankruptcy, and I must stress that it is not something you want to go through if you can avoid it, it's a complicated business and you may have to go to court. Citizens Advice has a comprehensive guide to bankruptcy that you should read before you make any decisions.

What is the base rate?

The base rate is the standard rate of interest that is set by the Bank of England, which all the other banks and lenders use as a guide when they set their interest rates. The Bank of England uses the base rate as a way to encourage spending and borrowing. It's worth being aware of the current base rate so you can tell whether the interest rate you are paying on your loan or mortgage is in line with general interest rates or is much higher or lower.

What is capital?

Capital is the money you have in your bank account (or your purse or under the bed) that you put into a mortgage. It's the lump sum you have before you borrow any extra. The term can also be used in a broader sense, to mean all of your wealth – i.e., your assets minus your debts.

What is compound interest?

It's basically when the interest you earn on your savings gets added to your total amount, so that you then start earning interest on a bigger amount than when you first started. (This is different from simple interest, which is calculated as a percentage of the original amount rather than a percentage of the total that is being topped up by interest each year.) The longer you leave your money in a savings account, the bigger it will grow and the more interest you will earn on it. Compound interest is a good thing with savings, less so with debts.

Equity loan

Also known as the Help to Buy scheme, this is where the government lends you a proportion of a property's price to help you buy it. Equity loans have been around for a while in various incarnations – some require you to be buying a new-build property, for example – so it's worth checking online at https://www.gov.uk/affordable-home-ownership-schemes/help-to-buy-equity-loan for the latest rules and conditions. An equity loan is a great way to get on the property ladder, but it will add an extra element to the house-buying process. Also, of course, it will need to be paid back, which can affect your ability to take your next step on the ladder if and when you want to.

Ethical investing

Some financial products such as ISAs offer 'ethical' options. This means that the fund or the bank you are dealing with will never invest your money in businesses that harm the environment, like deforestation of the Amazon, and won't have unethical practices such as the use of child labour. They don't always offer you the best interest rates but if you are looking for a clean conscience when it comes to saving and investing, then ethical products are for you.

What is excess?

Not as fun as it sounds! Excess is simply the amount of money you agree to pay if and when you make a claim on your insurance. So if you are claiming for a new windscreen and a new one costs £500, and you have an excess of £250 on your policy, you will need to pay £250 of the costs. The insurance company will pay the other £250. Low excess means you have less to pay in a claim situation but usually incurs higher overall costs for your insurance. They don't like to make it easy for you!

What is gross income?

Not anything disgusting, simply your income before costs are deducted. It's what you earn, not necessarily what you take home.

What is net income?

This is your income after tax, cost of goods sold, interest and any other expenses have been deducted – it's what you take home.

What is inflation?

It's a word for the general rise in the cost of living. Like how £5 used to go a lot further than it does now. That's inflation.

What's the Inland Revenue?

This is another term for HMRC (Her Majesty's Revenue and Customs). These are the people who work out how much tax to charge you and then do the charging!

What's interest?

It's a fee that you either earn (on your savings) or pay (on your debts.) If you put your money in a bank account, it's like you are lending the bank your money and they pay you interest for the privilege. They then lend your money to other people (borrowers) and charge them interest on their debts. The interest rate (the percentage) on savings is usually much lower than on anything you've borrowed, which is why you should never, as a rule, start saving until you are debt-free.

ISA

An Individual Savings Account, or ISA, currently lets you save up to £20,000 a year tax-free. There are different types of ISA – see pages 194 and 200 for more information.

Liquidity

Liquidity is a way of describing how easy it is to sell something (an asset) quickly for cash, without affecting its market value. Cash is the most liquid of all liquid assets. Houses have high liquidity, as does jewellery.

What is National Insurance?

This is the tax we pay to the government that pays for our pensions, benefits and the NHS.

Payday loans

This is a type of loan that you take out usually for a small amount of time, the idea being that you pay it back when you next get paid. They usually have very high interest rates and can lead to debt problems if you are not able to pay them back within the agreed time frame.

What is PAYE?

This stands for Pay As You Earn. It's just a term for the way you pay your tax if you are an employee. PAYE means your tax gets paid by your employer to the government at source, so you never see it. If you're self-employed, you have to send HMRC a tax return showing what you owe, and pay this tax to them.

What does peer-to-peer mean?

This refers to any company or network where you deal directly with the person you are selling to or buying from, cutting out the middleman and usually making it more financially rewarding for everyone involved. Selling platforms like eBay and Vinted are peer-to-peer marketplaces, as are Airbnb, SpareRoom and other owners-direct accommodation services. You can also lend and borrow money on a peer-to-peer model. As always, make sure you do your research and that any platforms you use are regulated by the relevant industry bodies.

What are premium bonds?

Premium bonds are a different way of saving money. Instead of putting money in a savings account or ISA, you 'buy' premium bonds. They don't earn you any interest but instead go into a prize draw with lots of different amounts of money to be won every month. It's a slightly different (and some think fun) way to save. Great if you like the idea of winning prizes and a nice gift for a new baby or a special birthday. But if you want to make your savings work and want some guarantees about how much you are going to gain over a year, premium bonds are probably not for you.

Scarcity impulse

Shops and market-sellers use the concept of scarcity to encourage us to buy things. As human beings we are programmed to fear scarcity and to 'stock up' in case we need things. Overriding your scarcity impulse is one of the hardest, but also most financially rewarding, things you can do as a shopper.

Secured loan

This is a type of loan where you have an asset (most commonly a house or a car) that you pledge as collateral against the loan. If you can't pay the loan back, the lender gets to keep your asset. A mortgage is the most common example of a secured loan.

Subprime lenders

Subprime lenders are financial companies that lend money to people who have low earnings and bad credit scores. Because this kind of borrower is assumed to be at higher risk of defaulting on their loan, interest rates are generally higher with subprime lenders.

What's a tax allowance?

This is the amount of money you are allowed to earn each year before you start paying tax. Also referred to as your Personal Allowance.

Index

Page numbers for glossary
entries are in *italics*

addiction 145–50

advice 167–9

Airbnb 115

allowances 229–35

anxiety 3–5, 17–18, 76, 243

apps 90–1, 232–3

APR *253*

arrears *253*

baby funds 195–9

baby showers 196

balance transfer cards
253–4

bank accounts 202, *254*

children's 227–8

joint 214–16

bankruptcy *255*

base rate *255*

beauty products 57–60

behaviour & money 135–
41, 145–50

birthday parties 67–70

Blue Light Cards 93

brand vs budget items
59–60

building societies *254*

cakes, birthday 69–70

capital *256*

car boot sales 62, 100–1

carbon footprint

clothes 54

energy 78–9

food 73
public transport 88
cars 80–2
petrol 81, 89
renting out 113–14
vs public transport 88
casual work 120–3
charity shops 62, 67
children
babies 195–9
bank accounts 227–8
clothes 64–7
eating out with 87
motivating 224–6
pacifying when out 29–31
parenting 206
parties 67–70
pocket money 229–35
and saving 222–35
saying no to 31
toys 29–31, 66
Christmas 66, 67
Citizens Advice 168
clothes

carbon footprint 54
children's 64–7
designer 52–3
fashion pieces 51–2
recycling 54
renting 53–4, 113
shopping for 50–3, 54–7
comparison websites 77, 82
compound interest *256*
consumerism 6
credit, availability of 5–6
credit cards 157, 162, *253–4*
balance transfer 165–7

death
future planning 212–14
ordering affairs 219–20
wills 218–19
debt 130–1, 157–69
advice 167–9
avoiding 161–6
and mental health 3–5, 158–61
paying off 162–5, 174–5

transferring 165–6

decluttering 101–2

delivery charges 94

Depop 109

designer outlets 52–3

discipline 186

discounts 90–2, 93–5

drinks out 27–8

eating out 35, 86–7

eBay 104–7

electronic equipment 83–5

emergency funds 175–9

energy efficiency grants 78–9

energy suppliers 77–8

environment. *see* carbon footprint

equity loans 194, *256–7*

ethical investing *257*

everyday expenses 37–8

excess *257–8*

expenditure & saving 25–7

Facebook Marketplace 108

family finances 206, 235

and children 222–33

financial security 208–11

future planning 212–21

feelings about money 139–41

food 69, 71–3

furniture 62

future planning 212–14

garage sales 104

garages, renting 112

gender stereotypes 208–9

gig economy 120–3

goals 179–86

setting 183–6

grants: home 78–9

gross income *258*

happiness 240–3

Help to Buy Scheme *256–7*

holidays, saving for 183–4

the home

decor 61–3

energy efficiency 78–9

insurance 82

makeovers 61–3

renting out 115–16

renting out rooms 110–11

utility bills 74–9

home ownership 191–4,
256–7

homewares 61–2

Hourly Rate Principle
34–8, 91, 139

household bills 74–9

income *258*

inflation *258*

Inland Revenue *258*

Instagram 56

insurance 82, 220–1

excess *257–8*

interest *255, 256, 259*

interior design 61–3

ISAs 200–1, *259*

Junior 94, 229

Lifetime ISAs (LISA) 194

journalling 133–4

leasing cars 81

life insurance 220–1

liquidity *259*

loans 150, 165–7

equity 194, 256–7

payday *260*

secured *262*

student 163–4

make-up 59

makeovers: home 61–3

marriage 217

mental health 3–5, 158–61

meter readings 78

Mind 168–9

mindset 24–5, 132–41

mobile phones 84–5

money 5–6, 135–41

mortgages 162, 176

motivation. *see* goals

mumpreneurs 123–6

nappies 199

National Insurance *259*

net income *258*

online shopping 37–8, 94

online surveys 117–18

parking spaces, renting 112

parties 67–70

payday loans *260*

PAYE *260*

PayPal 117

peer-to-peer *260–1*

pensions 187–90

performance psychology 181

personal allowance 256–7

personalisation 63

petrol 81, 89

phones 84, 85

photographs, taking 106, 116

planned ignoring 31

planning for the future 212–14

pocket money 229–35

pre-paid cards 232–3

premium bonds *261*

'premium for liquidity' 176

public transport 88

recycling: phones 84

renting out

   cars 113–14

   clothes 113

   parking/garages 112

   spare rooms 110–11

   your home 115–16

retail therapy 144

reward schemes 90–2

Samaritans 168

saving 13, 172, 203

   goals 179–86

   mindset for 24–5

   no spend days 42–5

scarcity impulse 142–4, *261*

school uniform 66, 67

second incomes 120–6

secured loans *262*

security 208–11, 240–4

self-employment 120–6

selling

   Make Money Day 116–17

online 104–9

unwanted items 98–104

shopping

addiction to 145–50

discounts 90–2, 93–5

Hourly Rate Principle 37–8

online 37–8, 94

reasons for 142–5

research 94

window-shopping 54–6

skills, assessing 208–10

small items

spending on 25–32

value of 36–7

snacks 35, 86–7

social media 16–17, 151–6

and self image 144–5

spending 25–32

addiction to 145–50

awareness of 33

no spend days 42–5

spending trackers 38–41

StepChange 168

store cards 92

stress 244

student loans 163–4

subprime lenders 157–8, 262

subscriptions 28–9

supermarkets 71

suppliers 77–9

support 45, 245–7

switching suppliers 77–8

tax allowances 262

tax: PAYE 260

technology 83–5

toys 29–31, 66, 67

tracking spending 38–41

travelling 27–8, 35, 86–8

utility bills 74–9

want or need test 137–9

water meters 78

wills 218–19

window-shopping 54–6

women & money 6–8

Acknowledgements

A huge, huge thank you has to go to Alan Samuel and Ange Walter at Spotlight Management. They have been incredible agents and have helped me immensely on this journey in creating Money Mum.

Also, to my literary agent, Lauren Gardner, at Bell Lomax Moreton, for helping me to meet Octopus and the wonderful Eleanor Maxfield for believing in me, along with her amazing team who share the same passion and drive as myself in getting this book out there.

I must also thank Sarah Thompson for bringing my voice to the page and helping me creatively write a book that I hope will empower everyone from all walks of life.

A massive thank you to all my loyal followers on Instagram and everyone that has supported in buying this book. Without you, this would not have been possible.

Lastly, my mum, dad and sister for being such a loving, supportive family. My amazing husband, Adam, for being there for me over the many hours of this book's creation as well my beautiful, loving children, Brody and Bronte who are my entire world.

I hope that you all enjoy the book, that it empowers you to save, brings people together and changes your mindset with regards to money.

Gemma
x.

Money Mum